For Heaven's Sake:

Finding Self Esteem at the Foot of the Cross

Jan Brunette

ISBN: 1-58851-078-6
PUBLISHED BY AMERICA HOUSE BOOK
PUBLISHERS
www.publishamerica.com
Baltimore

Printed in the United States of America

*To my husband, Duane, who taught me to look at life through
enlightened, enthusiastic eyes
To my eleven children and their spouses who provide
abundant joy and pleasure
To my grandchildren who enable me to view faith with
renewed creativity and trust*

Chapter 1

OUR FORTRESS -
A HAVEN OF SAFETY

We built the wall four feet high. Though low in comparison to our height, the goal of our determined spirits was thickness, not height.. Working feverishly, we packed and filled until the wall appeared about a foot thick. The enemy desired revenge. Adequate preparation and fortifying proved necessary. Finally trusting in our mighty haven, we hid behind it and quietly waited for an ensuing bombardment. Knowing that the mighty army on the other side intended to make a strong attack, we proceeded to supply ourselves with the proper ammunition and protection. Stacks and stacks of round spheres appeared behind our secure fortress. This would be the snowball fight of history. The challenge, though difficult, would be met. We trusted our fortress and our weapons. We would succeed.

Suddenly, the snowballs began soaring through the air and landing behind us. One after another they plopped and smashed. Glancing at my teammates, we began counting. Our strategy had begun.

Knowing their fortress had already been weakened from the previous day's bombardment and that no additional stockpile of weapons was made on their behalf, we assumed many of their snowballs would expire before long. Resolving to let them use many of their weapons first, we began a countdown. Gradually, they moved further and further away to secure adequate snow for their snowballs and their fort. Suddenly, with a warhoop only the other team members could understand, we began pelting their fort and them, not haphazardly, but methodically and intently. The time of capture arrived as our snowballs pelted and demolished and destroyed. Slowly, their fortress was chipped away. The challengers' heads became more and more visible. Their bodies, trying to sneak out for more snowball snow, met with attack, constantly followed by retreat. Before long, the victor remained obvious. Recognizing defeat, the other team raised their hands, and cheers of a job well done followed. Planning, preparation and lots of fun onour part resulted in an excited victory dance. The challenge had been met and won.

THE BATTLE IS REAL

The home was filled with strife and division. Anger, arguments, and destructive words appeared as a daily occurrence. Unhappiness abounded, and fears developed in many within the home. Could there ever be an end? This home manifested itself to others as a Christian home. Sunday worship was mandatory. The children attended a Christian day school. The parents and older children participated in many church activities. Yet, in their personal lives, Satan seemed to possess a strong grip. God didn't intend it to be that way, but over time, the weakness of some and the misguided thinking or habits of others created a home in trouble.

Shrouded in a mask of "religion", many homes today fit into that category. I believe it is more prevalent that we can ever imagine. Yet, until the problems become evident through abuse, divorce, or exposure, we remain unconcerned and oblivious to the entrance of Satan's influence into our homes. In addition, Christian neighbors molest and sexually fondle other children. Fathers, whether real, step or adoptive, mentally, spiritually, and sexually abuse their children, not to be discovered until many years later. Wives encounter the same type of abuse, often being told, "They deserve it." The wall of God's strength gradually becomes weakened and Satan's bombardment wins.

Yet, God promises many things to those who claim Him as their fortress and haven. Through His Spirit, I believe women can protect their home, both the building and the body. The walls of God's mighty fortress need to be built thicker. The weapons of the Spirit need to be claimed daily and fortified with His word. Though Satan may penetrate, he cannot succeed unless we allow him. We belong to the Risen Christ, and in Him is victory, regardless of our circumstances.

Also demolished is self-esteem. Whether through training or through a lack of Scriptural knowledge, many precious sheep - called women - suffer from a false sense of identity and misguided truth about their approach to self-worth. Belief in Satan's lies weakens our walls of peace with Christ, and the need for fortification becomes evident.

Strength comes through hiding behind the peaceful, serene security of God's love. The blessings of His strength and power follow. This promise of Jesus, when clasped firmly, can begin the process of healing in our lives: "'I have told you these things, so that in me you may have peace. In this world you will have trouble. But take heart! I have overcome the world.'" (John 16:33)

RESTORING OUR HOMES

"He who fears the Lord has a secure fortress, and for his children it will be a refuge." (Proverbs 14:26)

Kneeling before the Lord in submission, I desired the best for my family. Left alone after my first husband's death, I knew I could not adequately supply all the needs of my four small children. Wondering what would become of them and me, I inwardly screamed for God's help. He needed to provide and sustain all of us through our difficult months ahead.

God in His goodness never failed us. While all of us endured different aspects of grief and fear at different times, and the pain appeared obvious, healing prevailed. The march toward wholeness ended in Christ's victory.

But the pain didn't end there. Even after my remarriage to a friend in the ministry, difficulty scratched and gnawed its way into our lives. I heard somewhere that blended families don't blend, they collide. And that was definitely true of us. Different personalities, changed habits, and an unaccepted move dominated the foreground and created even more difficulties. The strains in our marriage were overwhelming, and often I felt Satan had more control than the Lord.

After finally understanding that an anointing of His Spirit needed revealing, I spent days and weeks walking through the house, claiming victory. I believed that the Lord truly existed in all our hearts and lives, but that Satan had masked and maneuvered his way into our presence. Refusing to allow him to devastate me through the circumstances, I vowed to do all I could to bring peace and to love even when it seemed impossible. I sought the Lord's presence daily and cried out to the Father for wisdom and guidance. The challenges didn't dissipate or disappear, but my thinking changed. Even when hurt, often crying many tears, I managed to place the situation into the nail-scarred hands of Jesus. I knew He loved me and would use all my situations and circumstances to strengthen me and create a Christ-likeness in me. Praying for the children eventually proved rewarding as I saw them also become strengthened and mature in spite of the inner and outer struggles they experienced. My husband gradually learned to understand his role in their lives and sought the Lord's strength in spite of the changes and behaviors with which he became accustomed. Today, six pastors and five

Christian day school teachers, (and eleven other active, devoted Christians) embrace our immediate family. Satan ultimately did not win. Determination and a resolute commitment to Christ in our marriage and family glued us together and enabled us to move onward in spite of all the challenges and difficulties.

Women, we can make a difference. We are worthwhile in the ministries of our families. The impact and deep abiding faith in the Mighty Fortress, who shelters us from Satan's stormy blasts, will guide, lead, and create a loving boldness against the evil that enters our families' lives.

In the process, His arms of sanctuary will provide a serene peace in the midst of muddied waters, a security in His power in the tumult of Satan's whirlpools, and ever-flowing comfort and joy amidst all temptation and sieges. In Christ Jesus is the Victory! "His commands are not burdens, for everyone born of God overcomes the world. This is the victory that has overcome the world, even our faith. Who is it that overcomes the world? Only he who believes that Jesus is the Son of God." (1 John 5: 3-5)

CALM IN THE STORM

"God is our refuge and strength, an ever-present help in trouble. Therefore we will not fear, though the earth give way and the mountains fall into the heart of the sea, though its waters roar and foam and the mountains quake with their surging...'Be still, and know that I am God; I will be exalted among the nations, I will be exalted in the earth.' The Lord Almighty is with us; the God of Jacob is our fortress." (Psalm 46:1-3,10-11)

The tiny infant nestled in her mother's arms. A head-full of dark hair covered her tiny crown. Miniature fingers and toes - all intact and perfect. While this was the fourth child of Martin and Clara, her entrance in this world left an indelible message on the heart of the mother. Through the night, Clara struggled with labor, for she gave birth before medications and pain relievers existed. Outside raged a terrible thunderstorm noticeable to Clara between the contractions. As the contractions and painful birth escalated the pain, so the storm created havoc outside. Wondering if either would end, Clara envisioned this child as her stormy one. When the tiny girl finally presented herself, Clara noticed the storm had completely subsided as well. Gazing at her new bundle of joy, Clara thanked God for the calm after the storm, both outside and in the birth of her infant daughter, Janet.

That daughter grew up as most children do. Storms raged in her life and eventually passed. But each event brought a new awareness of the calmness in Christ that evolves through the pain. The securing walls of love surrounding her became more visible with each lesson learned. The power of the Father's love, and His desire to provide inner peace and protection clarified itself with each passing day and event. While the walk within the world often seemed chaotic and confusing, yet within the fortress of God's all-sufficient mercy, the generous covering of His presence provided courage, joy, and strength.

I am that daughter. Recalling many events in my past, some more stormy than others, I would not change a moment of it. Through the pain and agony, I discovered a loving God who overwhelms me with the complete assurance that I am His. Nothing I can do will cause Him to love me more and nothing I can do will cause Him to love me less. I am accepted. I am precious in His sight.

But Satan loves to delude me and you into believing that things in our past or present can change that. Guilt, shame and regrets often stare us in the face - no thanks to Satan, and his army. But we must remember that even in our tumultuous seas, God is our solid mountain, our fortress, our haven of safety. There, He covers us with His love, and will do everything in His power to protect the faith we possess. He desires true joy that can exude only from Him. His joy becomes our joy. His strength becomes our strength. His goodness becomes our goodness. Not because we possess it on our own, but because Christ in us fills our void and insufficiency. In His eyes, because of the cross of Christ, He sees us pure, holy, and totally undefiled.

Our response is total surrender and submission to a God who desires our greatest good. Snuggling behind the solid, secure wall of God, our Fortress, He shields us and grants us the will, the desire, and the vision to serve Him and do His will. As our love for Him embraces our hearts, our attitudes and habits change. Guilt and shame are replaced with a clear conscience. Satan's lies are replaced with an honest heart. Doubt is replaced with a lively faith.

"'Be still, and know that I am God." Focus on the thought. Believe in God's divine providence and promise. He is your Fortress.

WHAT MORE CAN I DO?

Rambling down the highway, the children sang at the top of their lungs. They loved the children's tapes that were played, and they bounced and clapped as their hearts and bodies joined in the ecstatic joy of praising Him in song. Hours would pass quickly. Not only were their attitudes vibrant, but the pleasure of the hours spent in song also relieved me during the long driving process. What a pleasure to see love and laughter in action!

Never doubting His love during the process of grief in my life, I yet had misgivings about the approach He used in presenting that love. I ached inside from the loss of a husband of seventeen years and couldn't envision an end in sight. Loneliness dominated my life, even with the four precious, lively children that still absorbed and filled my time and energies. The weekends proved extremely painful as his absence from the children unveiled itself more predominately. At times, I wondered how God could possibly fix it. I hated the pain but had to believe in His power to heal.

Little did I realize that it would be through the avenue of praise that the pain would lift. Even listening to my children sing praises didn't bring about the connection I needed. Although I received an intense light-hearted spirit during those times, I failed to perceive the application of it in my own life of pain.

Fortunately, a friend recommended reading the book, <u>HEALING FOR DAMAGED EMOTIONS</u>, by David Seamonds. In this book, Mr. Seamonds presented the need for praise and described the positive effects of it. Clinging tightly to the promises of Scripture regarding praise, I began to dedicate my waking hours to determined praise thoughts. I once heard, "Your mind can only think one thought at a time." Accepting that as truth, I thought, "If I think praise, I can't worry. If I sing praise, perhaps the loneliness will dissipate. If I honor God constantly with praise when the stinkin-thinkin appears, then the negatives will disappear and positives dominate." In time, I realized this to be true. Praise does destroy the stronghold over my mind that Satan tries to grasp. It breaks his chains. It opens wide the door for God in His mercy to build that wall, that fortress around me.

Did I praise God for the pain? No. Did I praise God for my husband's death? Absolutely not. Did I praise God that my four young children were without a father? Hardly. But I did praise Him for His goodness, His power, His love and His strength in the midst of it. I did praise Him for the gentle touch of Jesus who understood my pain, and grieved with me. I did praise Him that in the process He was working a mighty act of creating Christ's character in me. Because of His love, He knew the journey would be worth the pain and the result powerful in His hands. Yielding to Him through praise became a fortress which still remains dominant today, for His furnace of love burned away my hardened spirit and created a spirit of abiding love and peace in Him.

"But I will sing of your strength, in the morning I will sing of your love; for you are my fortress, my refuge in times of trouble." (Ps. 59:16)

His presence touched me. His hope revived me. His unconditional love, even during my doubting, angry, frustrating times, totally covered me. His wall of protection, His fortress, remained steadfast. As I praised, questioned, trusted and cried, He remained secure. His need to stand back revealed an eternal surprise - Christ's life and goodness surfaced. Jan's strong will and dominance regressed. At the foot of the cross, I discovered my self-worth, for it rested not in myself, but in a sacrificial lamb that opened the doors of Heaven on earth for me. Praise God for His goodness! David A Seamands, Healing for Damaged Emotions Workbook(Wheaton, IL:Victor Books, 1992) p. 175

Chapter 2

LIGHT TO MY PATH -BRINGING LIGHT INTO A DARK PLACE

Heavy breathing awakened me. A rustling noise created a feeling of utter terror. Then silence. Dead silence. Maybe I only imagined it. The deep sleep and dreams may have aroused imaginations in my mind - imaginations that appeared so real that I felt wrapped in them. Before relaxing enough to doze off in slumber again, the sound of moving feet in my dark bedroom verified my fears. It instilled a shudder never experienced before. Looking at the bedroom door, I discovered it closed. Who could be in my bedroom? Was it an animal - but how could it get in? If it were one of my children, why would the door be closed? If a burglar, would I be raped or beaten or worse?

My husband died a year earlier. I had tried to accustom myself to sleeping alone, but often found it difficult. Noises in and around the house at night often startled me. But the sensation and reality of another presence in my room nearly froze me to the bed. Finally, softly and quietly I spoke, "Who's in here?" After a few seconds (although it seemed like hours), a voice timidly responded. "It's Trevin, Mom. I had a bad dream and I can't go back to sleep."

A rush of peace flooded my spirit. "But why did you close the door? And why didn't you wake me instead of slowly moving around the room? You nearly scared me to death", I chided.

His little eight year old voice tenderly responded, "Sorry, Mom. Sorry."

Touched by his apology and terribly relieved, I consoled him, gave him a gentle hug, and sent him back to bed. The dark night, previously filled with the fear of imminent danger, now contained the light of warmth and comfort. " Thank You, Lord. It could have been so much worse. Now, as you help me make it through the remainder of the night, in the morning grant me a rejoicing spirit as the new day dawns." Darkness often invades our lives. Shudders, tears, fears, and concerns for loved ones overpower. Although the Light shines, the darkness evident with each passing ache, pain, heartache, and decision creates a shadow that our spiritual eyes cannot detect. Just as the clouds block out the sun and alter the true visibility of the sun's radiance, so our darkest nights and loneliest days block out the brightness of the true reality of His Presence. Yet that Presence is there - never to be diminished or withdrawn.

Over time, many women discover feelings of inadequacy. Failed marriages, children who cause pain, verbal reminders of failures, abuse, and even spiritual depletion, instill in us constant reminders of our inability to succeed in things we do. Blame is the name of the game - whether from others or self-imposed.

I discovered several years ago, that one of Satan's greatest tools is shame. His deception creates a dark world that appears empty and void. It shadows and covers the true Light in our lives and allows him to jump up and down with glee as he sees us struggle with our personal self-worth. As a silent child moving quietly in the rooms of our minds, he creates fear, mental put-downs, and even, in some cases, terror. Satan's cruel darkness needs to be exposed in the Light of the precious Savior Jesus, who never desires or intends for us to feel shame or guilt. True conviction is important, as is repentance and forgiveness. Yet, Satan refuses to let conviction have the final word. Repentance and forgiveness finds no fertile ground as he constantly reminds and prods our minds with thoughts of the past, and covers it with shadows or clouds of despair.

Yet, the overpowering light of the constant, genuine tenderness in the eyes of Jesus whose love knows no limits, is available day and night - during good times and in times of terror. Picture Him grieving over your inability to accept the price He paid at Gethsemane and on the cross. He conquered shame. He erased guilt. He promises, "For I will forgive their wickedness and will remember their sins no more." (Jer. 31:34)

WALK IN THE LIGHT

"Submit yourselves, then to God. Resist the devil, and he will flee from you. Come near to God and he will come near to you." (James 4:7,8)

The greatest step toward freedom from darkness and walking in the light is submission. That means spiritual desire to surrender. It involves passing on all our fear of inadequacies, our blame, our shame, and our unforgiving hearts over to Him, and then leaving them at the foot of the cross. Relinquishing our need and desire for control creates resistance, for control is the one aspect of our lives onto which we tightly cling. Having the faith to let go of our "rights" for Him or anyone else eats away at our very being - especially if we have fought for those "rights" for many years already. Allowing someone else to lead and direct our life eats away at us as foreign and terribly frightening.

But the full light of Christ's presence will not remove the shadows until our heart, mind, and spirit open to His full radiance - the radiance of God's glory. (Heb. 1:3) In so doing, we discover that totally surrendering our lives into His loving, nail-scarred hands, brings freedom - not bondage. The chains of our past and our present pain fall to the lower dungeons of darkness, and we discover a world filled with His Light. In that Light, truth is revealed - not just the truth of our sins, but of His goodness, His forgiveness, His love, His abiding Spirit.

Accepting His radiance creates a radiance in us passed on from the inside out. "Those who look to him are radiant; their faces are never covered with shame." "Then you will look and be radiant, your heart will throb and swell with joy." (Ps. 34:5; Is. 60:5) The power of the Spirit overwhelms and creates a new being, one grounded and filled with His goodness. Faith and trust replace shame and blame and a thirst for the truth becomes our quest. The Morning Star rises in our hearts and new beginnings emerge.

SATAN HAS NO POWER OVER US

"Button, button, where's the button?" I called out. Slinking around the room, peaking on window sills, checking under cushions, even feeling on Mom's head, I determined to find the hidden button before my brothers and sisters. Instinctively, I moved to the piano and felt behind the music stand. "I spy!" I cried.

As moans and groans exuded from the others, I jumped up and down with glee. Now it was my turn to hide the button. Grasping the victory button tightly, I couldn't wait to be the next to challenge others.

Now picture Satan in this scenario. "Victim, victim, where's the victim?" he cries out. Slinking around the earth like a roaring lion, peaking into the hearts of the hurting, checking with his army for prey, feeling out openings of guilt even in comfortable places like our churches, he determines to find the hidden weakness in the very depths of our spirit. Finally, discovering that vulnerable spot, he pounces and shouts with glee, "I spy!"

As the Father in Heaven grieves, and tears fall from the eyes of Jesus, Satan rejoices in his victory button. Another child has fallen victim to his lies. Now he awaits the next step

- the next challenge. Satan's final desire - lost hope, lost trust, lost love.

God in His word lovingly shares these words, "Humble yourselves, therefore, under God's mighty hand, that he may lift you up in due time. Cast all your anxiety on him because he cares for you." (1 Peter 5:6,7)

Did you know these words were written before this: "Be self-controlled and alert. Your enemy the devil prowls around like a roaring lion looking for someone to devour. Resist him, standing firm in the faith, because you know that your brothers throughout the world are undergoing the same kind of sufferings."? (1 Peter 5:8,9)

Get on your knees, ladies! Get ready for your battle! Facing the Father whose overwhelming love amazes you, grasp the armor - the shield, the belt, the breastplate, the shoes, the helmet (Eph. 6:10-18). Claim victory over the terrible lies Satan uses in your lives. Pray for the light of the Gospel to flood into your spirit so that truth can prevail. Dig into the Word. Believe His promises of redemption and cleansing. "Then, the God of all grace, who called you to his eternal glory in Christ, after you have suffered a little while, will himself restore you and make you strong, firm and steadfast. To him be the power for ever and ever. Amen." (1 Peter 5:10.11)

Being blessed to visit the Sea of Galilee, I experience the "casting" of the nets. The picture in my mind forever serves as a reminder of the power of casting our cares on Him. Though the nets are heavy, these experienced fishermen forcefully and meticulously grasp the nets in their hands and arms. Then, with all the strength they can muster, they thrust the nets into the sea. They aren't just gently dropped over the side with a "plop". They are "cast".

The American Heritage Dictionary describes the word "cast" as, "to throw with violence or force, hurl, toss, fling; to throw off or away, to lose; to throw aside, dismiss, discard, get rid of; to overthrow, to defeat, as in wrestling." (p.209). Place any or all of these definitions into the verse found in 1 Peter and it spells victory - victory over worry, victory over cares, victory over Satan's lies and manipulations.

Besides humbling ourselves at the foot of the cross, we are expected to remain alert. Be on guard. Be prepared. That requires work, hard work on our part.

Being a lover of yard work, I often chose to be the individual who mowed our lawn when I was a young teenager. With a yard that spanned an acre and a half, the task often proved exhausting. Yet, I enjoyed the time spent outside, and I especially relished in the immaculate appearance of the lawn after completion.   The hard work took time.   It took perseverance. It required determination and a lot of sweat. Bracing ourselves for Satan's onslaught is no different. We must view the events, the thoughts, and the individuals through enlightened eyes. Only by loving and understanding the true Light, Jesus Christ, can we recognize the counterfeit when faced with it.

COME NEAR TO GOD

Filibuster Chatsworth sits on a small desk in my guest room. While cute and cuddly, he remains lifeless most of the time. But when he comes to life, children's eyes twinkle and their faces light up at his voice. Their little bodies jump up and down with excitement as he speaks with them. Adults respond with fascination and intrigue as they watch the responses between the two. While Filibuster Chatsworth is only a puppet (trademark of Boyd's Bears), his presence demands attention. The love he receives is overwhelming as children hug him, stroke him, and accept him as real.

The electrifying reactions of children to a seemingly lifeless bear creates pictures in my mind. Taking something that is seen, filling it with something unseen, and then speaking through another's voice, this creature takes on a personal attraction as nothing else can. Hearts are touched and memories of its message seldom go forgotten. It proves to be one of the greatest teaching tools I have ever encountered.

Yet God in His goodness uses His Spirit to create an even more unimaginable response through His children. Touched by the tender workings of the Holy Spirit, we become a special vessel for Him. As our hands lift toward Heaven in surrender and submission, exciting changes occur. Drawing into His presence, we become transformed. The inner darkness we experience discovers the light of His miracles in our life. As we ask God to fill us with the knowledge of Him through all spiritual wisdom and understanding, we begin to desire to live a life worthy of the Lord. Our thoughts change from ourselves to that of pleasing Him in every way. The drawing love that is generated in us enables us to bear fruit in every good work, growing in the knowledge of God. Yet even these miraculous changes cannot be attributed to us. The enabling Holy Spirit deserves the credit as we allow Him (the unseen) to work His will and way into our lives (from the inside). In the process, we become strengthened with all power according to that glorious might. But the divine purpose in all this is that we may have great endurance and patience, and joyfully give thanks to the Father, who has qualified us to share in the inheritance of the saints in the kingdom of light. (Col. 1: 9-12)

Drawing to the Father through the Spirit, our power source, opens our eyes to the kingdom of light - which is the absence of darkness. "For he has rescued us from the dominion of darkness and brought us into the kingdom of the Son he loves, in whom we have redemption, the forgiveness of sins." (Col. 1:13,14)

The closest correlation I can imagine concerning this thought is the birth of a child. After being encased in the womb for nine months, an infant, through much pain and travail on the part of both child and mother, escapes the darkened lodging of that womb to experience the brightly lit world of his parents. Everything is new and different - needs, feeling, emotions, desires for care. The same is true of the escape from the world of darkness - Satan's world - to that of the Risen Christ. As David said in 2 Sam. 22:29, "You are my lamp, O Lord; the Lord turns my darkness into light." Jesus Himself said, " I am the light of the world. Whoever follows me will never walk in darkness, but will have the light of life." (John 8:12)

But following Him requires a large measure of work on our part. It includes battles with Satan, praise for Christ's control and goodness even in the midst of pain and travail, time spent in Bible and prayer, searching, seeking, and asking which knows no end. We soon discover that each step eventually results in a shout with all the saints, "For with you is the fountain of life; in your light, we see light." (Ps. 36:9)

HE WILL DRAW NEAR TO YOU

"The precepts of the Lord are right, giving joy to the heart. The commands of the Lord are radiant, giving light to the eyes." (Ps. 19:8)

In speaking with a friend recently, I shared my awesome realization of His presence in many aspects of my daily life. The writing of this book proves to be no different. For many chapters, I struggled to take the time to sit at the computer, fearful that the words needed would fall silent. But time and time again, a thought, a phrase, a story popped into my head - not hours ahead, or days ahead, but as my hands centered on the keyboard.

Often, I would ask God, "What? You've got to be kidding. Where will that take me?" But obedient to His leading, I would begin typing. Often after the illustration stared me in my face on the screen, I would again ask, "Now what, Lord?" Although the next step often generated different responses, I could not help but tearfully respond, "Thank you, Lord. You have done it again. I praise You for Your goodness, for these are Your words, not mine. Give me the faith to never take credit for it."

I have so often heard authors say that a lightbulb goes off in their heads as they succumb to ideas, but I prefer to believe that He has drawn near to me in a very special way. The revelation of His goodness as I respond to obedience allows the Spirit to move in and through me. As a light to the eyes, He reveals all He can be.

God knows no limits. He is not confined to time and space. He is capable of doing all things for His children who seek His face and desire His will. Whether a working mother, a single parent, a stay-at-home mom, a grandmother, a single, a professional, God enters our spirit and strengthens us with power in the inner man. And that is a promise - not dependent on your ability, your accomplishments, or (your feelings of) self-worth. As He draws near to you through your study of the word, the celebration time spent with Him, and the inner desire to accomplish His will in your life, He will not disappoint you.

For us, it is only to remember that the cross of Christ is the freeing factor in all these things. Humbling ourselves at His feet is possible because of the price He paid on Calvary. Victory over Satan and his influence in our lives is broken because of the scarred, loving hands of the person of Jesus Christ. Drawing near to Him is accomplished through the workings of the Holy Spirit - His plan simply to engage in us that love of Jesus that is wider, higher, longer and deeper than ever imagined. The drawing of the Father's abundant love for us, an ecstatic privilege, nestles in the covering of the sacrificial, shed blood of His Son. For "the Son is the radiance of God's glory and the exact representation of his being, sustaining all things by his powerful word." (Heb. 1:3)

Now remember, dear sisters in Christ, that His next step for you is already complete, for "you are the light of the world...Let your light shine before men, that they may see your good deeds and praise your Father in Heaven." (Matt. 5:14-16)

Chapter 3

THE SALT OF THE EARTH -SPICING UP OUR LIVES THROUGH CHRIST

"Yuk," Trevin sputtered. "This pie tastes terrible."

Jennifer's eyes popped wide open. "What do you mean? I made it just like Mom's. It can't be that bad." Her voice gradually became shaky. She remembered her dedicated effort in making the pie. It hurt to think her brother disliked it.

"Mom," she pleaded. "Please try it and let me know it's O.K."

Unfortunately, I too could hardly swallow the delicious-looking pie. Trying to remain calm, I asked Jennifer to show me the ingredients she used in making the apple pie.

Pulling the spices from the cupboard, she handed them to me. Looking carefully at all of them, I reluctantly asked Jennifer, "Are you sure this is the brown spice you used?"

As she looked at the jar, she responded, "Yes, Mom, I used cinnamon. See, it says right here.......Oh no, I used cumin. I used the wrong spice." At first, tears started to flow, but when she looked at the grimaced face of Trevin, the tears changed to a smile. The smile then changed to laughter, to which we all joined.

Needless to say, the pie found its haven in the nearest garbage disposal, but the lesson learned proved priceless. Care must be taken in following recipes, for the wrong spice can destroy the usefulness of the finished product.

Jennifer, to this day, remembers the apple pie baked with cumin. But even more, she recalls the bitterness and the sour faces of those who sampled her wares.

I cannot help but wonder if many unbelievers face Christians today and inquire to what spices have been consumed. The grunts, the groans, the sour attitudes, the bitter spirits reflected in our faces, actions and reactions certainly indicate the flavoring that invades our heart and mind. Are we seasoned with hot peppers, syrupy sugar, or salt?

HOT PEPPER MENTALITY

Hot peppers create an atmosphere of animosity, anger, volatile justification, and consistent control. Inside us burns the need to fence in our environment and those around it. Fear often creates this "hot pepper" response as we enter circumstances beyond out control.Does this scenario sound familiar?

"Duane, I know you took the wrong turn. Why don't you go back and check it out?"

"No, we're fine. I know exactly what I am doing. There will be another place up here where we can turn and get back to the right street," responds Duane.

Fear of getting lost is foremost in my mind and I again say, "Duane, please go back. There is no guarantee that any street up here will get us back to where we need to be."

"Jan, just trust me. It'll be all right," he says calmly.

Seething inside, I sense the need to pound him over the head as I see turn after turn leading in the wrong places, some of them scary and dark. Inside I cry, "Lord, why won't he listen. It would have been so much easier to turn around and go back."

Fear absorbs me and anger starts to rear its ugly head. Finally, again, after realizing we are totally and completely lost, I harshly plead, "Duane, please stop and ask directions?" (Have you ever noticed that is not the suggestion they want to hear?)

Inwardly I shout, "Control, Lord. I want control! Just give me that steering wheel and we'll see who knows the best way out of here. If he doesn't do something - and soon - he may find that steering wheel around his neck."

Events from that point are generally downhill. Frustrated, frightened, and angry, I anguish over his foolishness. Finally arriving late, at least my first hour of our destination is ruined. (Please don't ask me how we got there. I was too angry to notice.) Any positive spices I possessed before leaving home succumbed to a "hot pepper" mentality. Regaining composure takes time and my unwillingness to surrender all things into God's hands appears evident.

Did you notice my need for control? "If only I were in charge, everything would have turned out better?" That, I believe, summarizes the greatest need for control. "No one will do it right." "It won't be done my way." "I won't be able to speak my piece - or maybe my whole mind."

At one point in our marriage, Duane resisted and resented my control over him. Not believing in my guilt, I began self-examination. In rehashing the events in question, I realized my control of Duane appeared in a secondary manner. While not desiring to control him, I did desire to control my circumstances. I stepped in, moved ahead, and carefully orchestrated the situations. But why? Ultimately, I was afraid of criticism, lack of acceptance, and fear of rejection. Having a deep need for his approval, I became devastated when I encountered differently. So I would try to do "everything" right, without realizing that by controlling the events, he also felt controlled.

That need for control remains with me unless I surrender "everything" into His loving hands and rest in the thought that His control over my life is perfect, loving and tender. Even when wrong turns are made by our spouses, our friends, or our children, God is still in control. "And we know that in all things God works for the good of those who love him, who have been called according to his purpose." Why?

So that we may "be conformed to the likeness of his Son." (Rom 8:28,29)

My husband's wrong turns in our travels (in the car or in life), my mistakes with others, the "foot-in-mouth-disease" I possess, will be used for good - not because I deserve it, but because He is a loving Father. He has called us into His Heavenly kingdom, covered us with the blood of His Son, Jesus Christ and granted us the power of His Holy Spirit to face all those need-controlling times of our lives. I have discovered that closing my eyes, taking a deep breath, and silently saying, "Jesus, I don't need to take control. Your control is sufficient. Help me to be still and quiet in Your love." The burden lifts and many "hot pepper" events are prevented.

"Oh, God, grant me the grace to love unconditionally and to yield my need for control over to You. I cannot do it without You. Amen"

SYRUPY SUGAR SPIRIT

My fingers appeared numb from scrubbing and waxing the kitchen floor, vacuuming the carpets, washing the fingerprint-stained walls, and dusting the furniture. With my parents gone for the weekend, I desired to surprise them with a polished, spotless home. Anxiously wringing my hands when their arrival appeared later than normal, I imagined all sorts of verbal pleasantries about my diligent labors. Gazing out the window, I jumped with a start when I finally saw the blue station wagon pull into the driveway.

Pretending that every aspect of the household shed only regular normalcy, I gave a nonchalant, "Hi, how was your trip?" as they entered through the door. Bubbling excitement and enthusiasm emerged from my parents and from my four younger brothers and sisters, who accompanied them on their weekend visit. The stories and experiences never seemed to end, but my inner spirit strongly desired for them to take notice of my labors. No one noticed. No one said a word.

"Oh, well," I thought. "As soon as everything settles down, they'll notice."

As luggage, purchased items, and the piles of toys, blankets, and pillows cascaded into the home from the car, I could tell my hard efforts would be less obvious with each passing wave of possessions. Order slowly replaced disorder - and sadly, so did the attitude of my spirit.

On the outside, I maintained my composure, yet on the inside, I cried and screamed for that attention I anticipated. "Mom. Dad. Don't you see it? Don't you see all the work I put into this? I worked so hard. Why aren't you saying something?"

My expectations never surfaced. Too much activity and the return of our home to its normal state prevented anyone from ever noticing. Nonetheless, I tried to remain cheerful and happy on the outside. In fact, over-compensating would be a better word. Flattery, compliments, and a quiet personality dominated and left my family wondering what event had created such a marvelous change in me. Little did they know that I chose to cover up my hurt with the opposite reaction, thus winning their gratitude through kindness rather than accomplishments. Their approval meant all too much to me.

While I finally recovered from the hurt of my own expectations, I could not help but wonder where I had failed. I had labored so hard, then tried to remain extra sweet in the aftermath, only to be met with confusion and rejection again.

This event entered in my pages of history as only one of many occasions upon which disappointment surfaced because of my expectations. Trying to please others, I worked hard, created controlled situations so as not to receive condemnation or criticism, and refrained from certain activities simply because I wanted others to accept me and award me the praise I felt due. When my expectations didn't surface, I often wept in the secrecy of my room or simply within, yet maintained an air of syrupy sweetness so as not to allow another moment of rejection to occur. My mind often chattered from the mistakes or lack of attention I received, and it often took days before the senseless, selfish chatter ended. Why did it matter so much? Why was I so desperate for the approval of others and so disappointed when I did not receive it? How could I break the cycle?

In time, I would learn that my struggle with acceptance created many disheartened and grieved feelings about myself. Putting too much weight on being "perfect" in the eyes of others, I became devastated when it didn't occur. Finally, I realized that I am already accepted exactly the way I am. Even though change is necessary in many areas, I know that in His own time and way, He will accomplish it through my willing spirit, the Holy Spirit and the loving tenderness of Christ. Wow! Can you imagine the devastation to my spirit if He revealed it all at once? He is so good in touching me one day at a time, one episode at a time. Also because of His cleansing breath on the cross, I am absolved of being perfect. You see, I AM perfect, but only because of Him. While my flesh struggles with being liked and popular, precious Jesus holds my hand and assures me that no one or no-thing can take His perfection away from me. God's ache in His heart is that we desire His praise, not the praise of men. (John 12:43) The need to pour syrupy sugar on others to gain their attention and approval ceases to dominate. His love takes over.

FLATTERY WILL GET YOU NOWHERE

Anger seethed inside them as He verbally slapped them in the face again. How dare this carpenter belittle them and embarrass them in public! He managed to hit the core of their evil hearts and they resented it deeply.

Leaving the temple, they marched outside to secretly meet with the Herodians, friends of the Roman rule. Although the Pharisees hated the Herodian's allegiance to Rome, they needed ammunition and power on their side. With their disciples clustering around Jesus, they proceeded with their charade. Appearing pious and sincere, syrupy sugar flowed from their mouths. "Teacher," they said, "we know you are a man of integrity, and that you teach the way of God in accordance with the truth. You aren't swayed by men, because you pay no attention to who they are." (Matt. 22:16)

Devious and deceptive, their motive shone clearly in the all-knowing spirit of Jesus. They desired entrapment, not truth.

"Tell us then what is your opinion? Is it right to pay taxes to Caesar or not?" they questioned. (Matt. 22:17) Hoping to throw Him off-center, they knew any answer would cook His goose. If He answered in favor of paying the Romans, the Jewish people would be incensed. If He answered against paying the Romans, the Herodians would immediately report Him to the Roman authority. They perceived it as a no-win situation.

Unfortunately, to their dismay, as many times before, He called a spade a spade. First, He called their bluff by catching them on their attempts to trap Him, and secondly, He called them by their true name - "hypocrites".

Jesus in no way succumbed to their flattery. He rested secure in His Heavenly position and spiritually discerned their words as lies and deception. Facing them head on, He conquered, leaving them retreating with their tails between their legs. (Matt. 22:15-22)

We say, "But He was God. It was easy to detect the evil in their hearts." And you are correct, for verse18 states that fact. But we too have that same Holy Spirit within us, granting us the ability to discern and detect truth from lies. Unfortunately, all too often our self-esteem rests in the "flattery" of others, thus hindering the reception of the Holy Spirit's voice. We need to place His approval as foremost, and to pray for our hearts to listen to His truth, not the lies of others.

Not all flattery placed on our plate is negative. God Himself flatters us constantly. "I have redeemed you; I have summoned you by name; you are mine...You are precious and honored in my sight." (Is. 43:1,4). "I am honored in the eyes of the Lord and my God has been my strength." (Is. 49:5) "I have engraved you on the palms of my hands; your walls are ever before me." (Is. 49:16) "How great is the love the Father has lavished on us, that we should be called children of God! And that is what we are!" (1 John 3:1)

Amazing love and acceptance flow from His Spirit. An "anointing from the Holy One" pours over our lives. (1 John 2:20,27) The esteemed position of "Christ's ambassador" remains sealed in our hearts as we serve Him daily. (2 Cor. 5:20) With all these titles and blessings, why would flattery from others even hold heart and home in our spirits? Our earthly position holds little weight when we understand the kingly position into which we are placed through Christ.

Examine the flattery of others as you remember these verses:

"He who rebukes a man will in the end gain more favor than he who has a flattering tongue." (Pr. 28:23)

"May the Lord cut off all flattering lips and every boastful tongue that says, 'We will triumph with our tongues; we own our lips - who is our master?'...The words of the Lord are flawless, like silver refined in a furnace of clay, purified seven times. O Lord, you will keep us safe and protect us from such people forever." (Ps. 12:2,6,7)

Remember - Christ cannot receive the glory when we are hoarding it for ourselves.

SALT - THE SPICE OF LIFE

"For I resolved to know nothing while I was with you except Jesus Christ and him crucified. " (1 Cor. 2:2)

Several years ago, a religious announcer for a local radio station asked me to write and deliver one minute devotions. Swelled with pride, I consented. Several months after airing, I again received word from her for a similar request. Though thrilled, I stopped short when she added, "I do ask that you leave out the name 'Jesus' since these devotions are for all religions." Realizing I couldn't omit His precious Name, I responded, "I can't do that." In that declaration, instead of feeling sadness over the loss of radio time, I experienced wonderful joy and excitement in acknowledging Christ as first in my life. My life spread salt that day as I declared my allegiance to Jesus.

Salt - preserving, cleansing, purifying, lasting. As part of the Old Testament burnt and grain offerings, God commanded its use. Just as He desired the sacrifice to be palatable and tasty, so He looks at us and asks, "Are they my true salt? Do they flavor and season the lives of those around them?"

The gospel of Christ becomes the truth in our lives. His presence fills us with peace and embraces our will and desires. Yearning to share that gospel, we cry out to His Spirit for ways in which we can spread that gospel to others.

"You are the salt of the earth. But if the salt loses its saltiness, how can it be made salty again? It is no longer good for anything, except to be thrown out and trampled by men." (Matt. 5:13)

Christ not only grants us the gospel to share, He gives of His Salt. When we hold tightly to Him and focus our eyes directly on Him, He becomes the direction, the hope, the flavoring, the spice we pass on to others. We in turn become the salt that is cast onto others. Whether through sacrifice, through words, through kindness, or through forgiveness, that salt is spread in hopes of creating a more palatable, more appealing life to others. When we enter the lives of others, God says, "You are there to add much needed spice to their life - not pepper, not syrupy sugar but salt. No matter how difficult the person, how trying the circumstances with that person, we need to apply the lasting, cleansing gospel to their bitter, lonely existence.

But without Christ as our center, our focus, we become flat and useless. Our words and actions are cast off as a joke - useless garbage. If we say we love the Lord but cheat on taxes or on our husbands, words of the gospel appear clouded and even dirty. If we profess God's goodness but are unkind, hateful, and unforgiving, our salt is cast on the ground, totally useless. God's gospel is discarded and perhaps a laughing stock to those to whom we profess that gospel.

Purification was demanded of the Old Testament sacrifices. So purification is expected of His followers. "Everyone will be salted with fire. Salt is good, but if it loses its saltiness, how can you make it salty again? Have salt in yourselves, and be at peace with each other." (Mark 9:49,50)

The fire of sacrifice is painful. It is demanding. It is powerful. In the process, we realize our helplessness and recognize our deep, intense need and desire for God's loving presence. Willing to deny self, we take up that cross He awards us and rejoices in our suffering for Him. Knowing that in the trial, Christ-likeness glows more abundantly, we willingly yield to the fire. Accepting it is part of our need to be salty, and we cry, "It hurts, Father, and I hate it, but I know you are creating in me the person you desire me to be - one that is useful, palatable, and at peace with others. The best part is that you will love and accept me through the refining process. For You love me not because of who I am or even whom I will become, but because of Whose I am. Only in Christ can I be the salt of the earth. Only then can my conversation be "full of grace, seasoned with salt, so that (I) may know how to answer everyone." (Col. 4:6)

"Yes, Jesus - I decided to know nothing among the masses except You. If I cannot share of You, of Your gospel, of Your love, my salt is wasted. With You I spread the taste of You to all with whom I come in contact. Through Your Spirit, the words penetrate. With You, the salt is purifying, refining, and cleansing. May I never forget to keep my eyes on You, the true Salt."

Chapter 4

JESUS, THE ROCKSOLID GROUND TO STAND ON

The man's rough hands gently rubbed the jagged rock. His eyes, fixed on its form, studied every crack, bump, and groove. Day after day, hour after hour, he embraced the rock, measured it and prayed over it. Only he could understand the value of this apparent, useless, dirty piece of stone. With a vision in mind, he evaluated the priceless treasure hidden inside and determined it worth the effort.

Finally, the day came for him to begin the molding, the shaping, the creating. The masterpiece gradually emerged, but only after hours, days, months and years of demanding effort, marred hands, and backbreaking labor. Although the man often desired retreat from his labors, he knew the rock would remain true and steadfast. Struggling with depression, the artist managed to force himself to face the rock one more time - the rock always there, always waiting. Weary of the journey, he wondered if the rock was worthy of his intense creative juices.

But the rock, standing faithful and secure, allowed the man time to discover the preciousness of his beauty. When the time for the unveiling arrived, the man stood back and marveled, not at his own skills, but at the glory and beauty of the rock itself - for without the rock, his own creative hands would have had no value or worth. The beauty rested in the rock - the strong, true, faithful rock.

SECURE

Over time, the strain of her disease and the days of confinement shattered her emotions. Tumbling into despair, she stared at the full bottle of pain pills sitting on her table.

"Lord, I'm tired of the pain and loneliness. It just never goes away," she wept. She picked up the bottle with her shaking hand, she quietly whispered, "God, please show me my life is worthwhile. Otherwise, these pills will be my comfort and consolation."

In that instant the doorbell rang. Startled by its timing, she placed the bottle back on the table and stumbled her way to the front door. There stood her long-time friend and pastor. Upon entering the door, he sensed a desperate look in her eyes. Gently grasping her hands, he prayed, listened, and cried with her.

"Mary, please understand this. God loves you so much that he planted in my heart the need to stop in and see you today. I was not scheduled until tomorrow, but God's tender Spirit pushed, prodded, and motivated. Rest and peace of mind would not come until I got in that car and pulled into your driveway. Now, I praise God that I listened to His voice. Jesus understands your struggle with pain and deeply desires your presence here on earth much longer."

With that confirmation, he left her with the following words, "He alone is my rock and my salvation; he is my fortress, I will not be shaken. My salvation and my honor depend on God; he is my mighty rock, my refuge. Trust in him at all times, O people; pour out your hearts to him, for God is our refuge." (Ps. 62:6-8)

What is the similarity between the artist in the first story and this woman? What connects these two so closely?

Pain, struggle, brokenness, despair - all common threads. A rock - a solid, secure foundation - a patient, immovable presence in their lives.

So often we become dismayed and choose to blame God when difficult circumstances enter our lives. "A God of love and compassion would not have permitted my son to die." "He could have healed my mother." "He should have turned away the tornado that destroyed my home."   Questions regarding His goodness in the midst of crisis pound through our brain like a sledge hammer. How dare He inflict so much pain on someone He loves!

"From the ends of the earth I call to you, I call as my heart grows faint; lead me to the rock that is higher than I. For you have been my refuge, and a strong tower against the foe. (Ps. 61:2,3)

That crisis, that pain, the encounter with despair all have a loving, eternal purpose. His wisdom far exceeds ours. In His heart, He desires that the current suffering be turned into His construction. As the edges of the rock are hewn away, we see Him more and more for who He is - a loving, tender, compassionate but firm, solid rock on which to place our lives and our trust. He won't crumble under us. He won't fall apart. But as we touch, chip, and smooth away the outer edges of our false beliefs of who He is, the more His love comes into view.

Jesus - His ultimate goal! He wants us to see Jesus. The nail-scarred hands, the loneliness, the agonizing fear over His own physical and spiritual torture, the rejection, the love, the forgiveness, the tender compassion for His own family. He epitomizes all of them. There is no event - past, present or future - that He has not experienced. He understands our despair and He loves us through them. He remains solid and secure for He is the Rock that hides us within Himself. He pulls us toward His very heart in the midst of the pain. While not always eliminated, it is shielded and covered with His love. Placing our feet firmly on Himself, our Solid Rock, He reveals hope and grants peace.   Strength to endure becomes evident as we face the muck and mire, one day at a time.

Both the artist and the sweet Christian woman in our story know the agony of enduring. It wasn't easy, nor did it miraculously disappear. But in the process, the Rock emerged in their lives, strong, secure, and trustworthy.

"I waited patiently for the Lord; he turned to me and heard my cry. He lifted me out of the slimy pit, out of the mud and mire; he set my feet on a rock and gave me a firm place to stand." (Ps. 40:1,2)

COME TO THE LIVING STONE

The stone rolled back and forth from the force of the waves. It nestled among hundreds of other rocks, yet attracted my attention. Picking it up for further examination, I noted that its color reflected glistening greens rather than the grays and browns of the small rocks surrounding it. Holding it in my hand, I felt determined to understand its significance to me.

Suddenly, I realized that the tiny rock in my hand was not a rock at all but rather a small piece of glass. Due to the constant motion of the waves, rubbing rock against rock, this once jagged piece of glass smoothed to a glistening, lovely "rock". Attracted to it by His Spirit, I accepted the illustration as one sent from Him.

Weary of spirit and lonely in heart, I needed to understand the purpose for my grinding life. With the death of a father and husband within three weeks time, the move to another location, the returning to a full-time job and the constant care of four young children, I often felt faint-hearted and in despair. By the Spirit's strength, I understood that God had a purpose, but my mind could not understand why it had to hurt so much and last so long.Holding the small piece of glass in my hand, tears welled in my eyes. I now understood. The rough edges of my life needed polishing. In order to shine with the radiancy of Christ's love, the trials and pain served His purpose in assisting that development. As Christ allowed the irritations and difficulty to rub against me, He knew that in time, I would not only shine for Him, but rest secure in His love - the solid Rock on which to stand.

Recalling the events of the months and years to come, I wallowed in His strength, even when the "rubbing" seemed the worst. His presence as my Living Stone reassured me. "As you come to him the living Stone - rejected by men but chosen by God and precious to him - you also, like living stones are being built into a spiritual house, to be a holy priesthood, offering spiritual sacrifices acceptable to God through Jesus Christ...But you are a chosen people, a royal nation, a people belonging to God, that you may declare the praises of him who called you out of darkness into his wonderful light." (1 Peter 2:4-5,9)

Irritations rub us the wrong way - but praise be to God for His goodness! In the precious, tender hands of the Crucified Savior, the rubbing produces stones that create special, unique individuals. Broken but blessed, a new awareness of His presence draws near.

As Jesus was "chosen by God and precious to him", we also are His chosen and precious stones. And it doesn't end there. Because of the wearing down of the old man and the replacing of the new, we, through His Spirit, become a "spiritual house" and a "holy priesthood". Can you imagine? We take on His likeness. We radiate - like a furnace blazing forth with His love and His power. We take on His righteousness, His fruit of "love, joy, peace, patience, kindness, goodness, faithfulness, gentleness, and self-control." (Gal. 5:23) We belong to Him. We live in Him and He in us. (John 17:20-23) "How great is the love the Father has lavished on us, that we should be called children of God! And that is what we are! (1 John 3:1)

Being privileged to be His child, we respond to that blessing "by offering spiritual sacrifices, acceptable to God." We do so in three ways. First, "we declare the praises of him who called you out of darkness into his wonderful light." (1 Peter 2:9) Secondly, we "love one another, for love comes from God. Everyone who loves has been born of God and knows God...if we love one another, God lives in us and his love is made complete in us...If anyone acknowledges that Jesus is the Son of God, God lives in him and he in God. And so we know and rely on the love God has for us. God is love. Whoever lives in love lives in God, and God in him." (1 John 4:7,12,15-16) Lastly, we obey and follow His commands. "This is how we know that we love the children of God; by loving God and carrying out his commands. This is love for God; to obey his commands. And his commands are not burdensome, for everyone born of God overcomes the world. This is the victory that has overcome the world, even our faith. Who is it that overcomes the world? Only he who believes that Jesus is the Son of God." (1 John 5:2-5)

What a privilege to bear His name! What an honor to serve Him in unselfish dedication. With burdens lightened by the Risen Christ, we gladly bear the burdens of others. We follow in the train of the saints in the past, committing our lives to His will and His commands, even if it often means rejection, trials, suffering and the like. Resting our rough edges at His feet, we rely on the Living Stone to polish us and always to remain firm and solid. On that we stand secure.

Chapter 5

THE LIVING WATER -NEVER ENDING SOURCE OF GOODNESS

The dry, parched river-bottom cried for water to flow through it. The smallest pools gave little hope of existence to the few remaining tadpoles and minnows. The leaves of the trees on the river bank seemed to stretch Heavenward, as if crying out to God in Heaven for relief from its thirst. The river which once teemed with life, now appeared lifeless and void of hope for its future.

Yet only a few miles away, another river exploded with activity. Fish, crabs, and all manner of life exhibited itself. The trees nearby appeared healthy and vibrant, leaves dancing in the sun as if praising God for the abundance of water offered. Fresh, clear water provided hope for this river's future.

The difference rested in the source. The first river found its supply from other lakes and streams that were also drying up from the prolonged drought. The second river flowed faithfully as a deep, underground stream supplied water endlessly and dependably. One brought life, the other death.

In today's world of materialism, wealth, and pleasure, many "streams" are drying up. Believing that things of this world can provide happiness and contentment, our lives become absorbed with gaining more and more. Credit cards are maxed out, debts overflow, and strife overwhelms in the family. Many homes are broken and in disarray because one or both spouses cannot curtail their desires and spending. It is not unusual for families to be over $30,000 in debt just in credit cards. The days of "what I want, I get - NOW" is prevalent. It's leading to dry rivers - with no hope of life, no hope of escape.

Thinking about the effects of dry, lifeless river beds reminds me of a trip we took to Gatlinburg, Tennessee. Traveling through the beautiful Cherokee National Forest, the awesome beauty entranced me. The mountain streams, crystal clear and consistent, paralleled the road. Though winding and slow moving, it marched onward toward its destination. Rhododendrons and dogwoods, fed by the same waters that filled the stream, abounded and bloomed profusely. Life revealed itself.

Suddenly, in the back of our car, came a whimpering sound from Trevin, our son. "Mommy, I don't feel so good." No sooner had the words slid from his mouth than we heard a stagnant, erupting stream of disgust. Having eaten a breakfast of cereal and milk, followed by a nap in the moving car on a winding road, havoc surged within his stomach. Needless to say that breakfast returned again, only to remind us of what a healthy stream is not. The odoriferous and wafting smell created such an uproar with the other three children that we knew a pit-stop was needed. Parking next to the free-flowing stream, they indulged in its freshness while Tom and I proceeded to clean up the mess and air out the car. Our gratefulness for clear, sweet-smelling streams appeared as refreshing as Heaven itself.

If, in our lives, we seek dry river beds, such as the joys of this world, eventually it will force us to erupt in hopelessness, despair and depression. The result is stagnant, unhealthy conditions that may be worse than the dry bed itself.

For a time in my life, I considered my self-esteem to rest in what I wore and how I looked. Constant trips to stores only created more hunger for the things I saw. So many pretty clothes, so much to make me beautiful - or so I hoped. Besides I was getting tired of the chores at home, the bottles, the diapers (and the effects of it!). Buying "things" made me feel good about myself - at least for a while. Yet, tomorrow I needed the same boost again. Discontentment with what I had and a restlessness to get out and shop created unhappiness and loneliness. Yet no amount of buying satisfied. I always wanted to do it again.

Eventually, I realized they were only stagnant waters - with nothing permanent to create the joy within that I desired. It wasn't until enduring a devastating time in the "pits" that my heart opened to the true Living Water. Christ opened a gushing flow of goodness, peace, joy, and comfort achieved only as I entered His presence in total and complete submission. Accepting my own helplessness and my need for a permanent solution to the inner void, Jesus filled me to overflowing with all the blessings of Heaven. His consolation and forgiveness in my life fed my deep inner longings. I realized that nothing on earth could grant me relief, for my rewards were not earthly (although I am truly blessed with that). The joy-filled rewards emerged as eternal - Heavenly. His steady stream of spiritual empowerment provided ultimate and lasting contentment and peace.

While I still desire to appear well-dressed and attractive, it is not to feed my own personal self-esteem. It is because I desire to remain attractive as I represent Him in this world. It is not dependent on the latest styles or the name-brands. I seldom enter major department stores any more. Regular trips are a no-no, for I realize it effects my contentment level. Accepting the self-esteem that rests in the Living Water, Jesus Christ, I endlessly and, with rejoicing, seek security and joy in Him.

"They feast on the abundance of your house, you give them drink from your river of delights. For with you is the fountain of life; in your light we see light." (Ps. 36:8,9)

LEARN FROM THE DEER

With tongue dragging, Sandy, our dog, desired a watery reprieve from the long afternoon in the hot sun. Having raced, played games, and dodged our attempts to capture her in play, she was left with an overwhelming thirst. Recognizing her need for replenishment, a large bowl of water became a priority. Lapping furiously, she drank from the welcomed supply. Then, completely refreshed, she was ready to spring into action again. The transformation in her energy elevated from fatigue to boundless energy in a matter of a few minutes."As the deer pants for streams of water, so my soul pants for you, O God. My soul thirsts for God, for the living God. Where can I go and meet with God.?" (Ps. 42:1,2)

Animals crave water - fresh and living water. As our dog Sandy panted at the absence of it, so a deer does the same. It even stretches out its neck in search of it. At times of severe drought, when water hides in lonely locations, the deer must search long and hard to discover a relief from its distress. Its sole purpose - to find water. When found, drinking fails to cease until the thirst is quenched. Yet the thirst for that fresh water creates a new search tomorrow.

Our parched soul craves God's presence. In despair, in loneliness, we thirst for the streams that are endless, that satisfy our parched and thirsty soul. Realizing that nothing on this earth can soothe the dryness we experience within, we seek God. We desire nothing but His presence. In our search, we indulge in one lap of water after another. As we daily drink from His streams of love, the thirst for His presence becomes ongoing. Each lap that we take of His flood of grace - through prayer, through meditation, and through Bible study - satisfies, yet creates a yearning thirst for more. A deep, abiding love evolves as we discover an endless supply from an abundant

Thirst-Quencher. Apart from Him, there is no respite. At His streams of abundance, we are satisfied.

Through the Living Water, another day of pain becomes easier. One more bout with loneliness succumbs to peace. Grief is assuaged. Swallowing His goodness and tasting the refreshment given by His Spirit, our spirit experiences unimaginable relief and quenching of thirsting spirits.

But often this requires sitting on the bottom - in a pit without a way out. Looking into the Heavenlies, panting for a respite from the burning hurt within, God reaches down and promises to provide an endless supply of living water. "I open my mouth and pant, longing for your commands. Turn to me and have mercy on me, as you always do to those who love your name...Make your face shine upon your servant and teach me your decrees." (Ps. 119:131-132,135)Revived one day at a time, praise follows. "Why are you downcast, O my soul? Why so disturbed within me? Put your hope in God, for I will yet praise him, my Savior and my God...By day the Lord directs his love, at night his song is with me - a prayer to the God of my life." (Ps. 42:5,8)

Circumstances may not change, but the attitude of our heart does. His presence changes the course of our broken hearts and dreams, as His endless streams pour into ours. Content with His presence, we desire His will in our lives. His radiant streams flood from our faces as a visible pronouncement of His goodness. "Those who look to him are radiant; their faces are never covered with shame." (Ps. 33:5) The awesome God deserves praise and honor as the ever-present flow of His Spirit washes through us.

SATAN'S DECEPTION

One of the deepest ravages of our soul is guilt. Satan loves to pound us endlessly and mercilessly. Another that is close is anger - resulting from hurt, fear, or severe disappointment. Bombarding our mind with negative thoughts, we take our eyes off the stream and stretch out our neck toward stagnant waters.

I can remember days that I cried to the Lord, desiring negative thoughts to dissipate. I would ask, "How can I rid myself of them and return again to the fresh spring? What is the secret?"

Satan loves to convince us there is no freedom from his constant mental bombardment and input. And all too often we believe Him. We blame ourselves for the terrible thoughts that exist, thus creating more feelings of guilt. But Christ desires our freedom from even the thoughts that poison our minds. In Him is victory. But what can I do to inherit it?

I believe there are some very wonderful steps to procuring that freedom. But practice and sacrifice must dominate.

First, enter the Lord's presence in complete humility and seek His face through prayer and Scriptures. Notice I didn't say, "Seek a solution to the problem." I said, "Seek His face." When you discover Christ, you automatically have the solution.

Second, confess your own sins and eliminate the blame that points its finger at the other person. Your own personal healing cannot take place until you accept responsibility for your own feelings and actions.

Third, ask God to reveal the area(s) of growth you need to encounter. Seek to discover the habit, the sin, the improper attitude that needs correction in your own life. It is so easy to fault the other person, and maybe justifiably so, but God is in control of them and their conditions. Trust Him to work mighty, Heavenly miracles, in you first, and then leave the rest to Him.

Fourth, offer a sacrifice of praise - and often in extremely difficult situations, it will be a painful sacrifice. But trust in His streams of living waters enough to believe that through praising Him, a gamut of negative feelings and emotions will fall as chains binding us tightly.

Even as I write this section, I encounter a bombardment from Satan. To overcome, I will claim the victory through Christ by tapping into His source of refreshing streams and follow the steps above. And as His Spirit supplies His stream of living water, I will experience a renewal of the mind. I know - because I've experienced it before and I believe in His promise to evacuate Satan's thoughts from my mind and to fill it with positive things. Praise will end the struggle - praise will restore my mind to His Heavenly thinking. "Set your minds on things above, not on earthly things. For you died, and your life is now hidden with Christ in God...Let the peace of Christ rule in your hearts, since as members of one body you were called to peace. And be thankful." (Col. 3:2-3,15)

The Scripture mentioned above is followed by the verse, "Let the word of Christ dwell in you richly as you teach and admonish one another with all wisdom, and as you sing psalms, hymns and spiritual songs with gratitude in your hearts to God." (Col. 3:16) Christ must be deeply implanted within each of us through fellowship with other believers and through His word in order to resist the onslaught of Satan. Only in Christ and through His Spirit can we hope to overcome. Void of power in resisting on our own, we must rest - not splash violently - in His mercy streams as we cry out, "Get behind me Satan! You are a stumbling block to me; you do not have in mind the things of God, but the things of men." (Matt. 16:23) Satan must flee. Christ will win.

But never under-estimate Satan; he will not give up. The subject will come up again and you will need to do battle again. When it occurs, remember God's promise, "If only you had paid attention to my commands, your peace would have been like a river, your righteousness like the waves of the sea." (Is. 48:18) God grieves when we fail to drink of His living water through obedience and submission. But as endless as the rivers, His love will pour forth and, as constant and predictable at the waves, His mercies will not fail those who turn to Him in love.

THE SOURCE

Feverishly digging in the dirt, I hoped to find it. Groping in the dark, I desired to discover it. Flailing in the sea of muck and mire, I aimed my outstretched arms toward it.

What was I truly seeking? Where could its discovery lead me? Only another individual having scratched the sides of a pit themselves could understand my frustration. I scratched and groped and flailed for an understanding of God's plan in my life. Finally, in sheer weariness, I gave up. Settling in despair, I cried, "Dear God, help me. I encounter so much pain and fear but yield it all to You. I can't fix it, Father! You must do it for me."

In my barrenness of soul, His refreshing Spirit began to invade my pain and procure an exciting new dimension of love and peace. Day after day, He guided, inspired, and engulfed me with love beyond comprehension, and restored me to a unique relationship with the Lord of Heaven and earth. Fear began to slowly dissipate. Touches of His presence flowed. The Holy Spirit fulfilled His calling in my life by giving me a new vision and hope for the future. Abundant life, once a promise, was now at work in me.

Although saved by His grace since childhood, I now deeply understood the overpowering purpose of the Holy Spirit. Refreshed, I recalled the words of Jesus, "'If anyone is thirsty, let him come to me and drink. Whoever believes in me, as the Scripture has said, streams of living water will flow from within him.' By this he meant the Spirit, whom those who believed in him were later to receive." (John 7:37-39)

Storms have come and gone. Mountains and valleys still invade my life. But a constant remains. The Holy Spirit continues to provide an endless supply of His power, His goodness, His strength, His forgiveness, His boundless joy. While the valleys are difficult and often require purification and refinement, His Spirit never fails to pour water over the hot metal and cool it with His refreshing peace. Jesus once said, "The Counselor, the Holy Spirit, whom the Father will send in my name, will teach you all things and will remind you of everything I have said to you. Peace I leave with you; my peace I give you. I do not give to you as the world gives. Do not let your hearts be troubled and do not be afraid...In this world you will have trouble. But take heart! I have overcome the world." (John14:26,28; 16:33)

His Spirit confirms my loving relationship with Jesus Christ, the Lover of my soul. His Spirit brings things to my remembrance as I grope through life. He tells me, "Jan, you are special. You are loved - so much that an eternal, painful sacrifice was made in your behalf. You are now cleansed. You are now free to serve the Living God, not out of obligation, but out of deep love. I will not forsake you. I will not leave you. I always have your best interest at heart." His mission in me was to procure a Christ-like beauty - a beauty that could not and would not fade.

As I drink from His source of endless love - His source of total acceptance- I discover that the stream does not stop within my spirit and become a stagnant pool. The life through the "streams of living water" flows gently through me to others. I cannot feel it. In fact, it is in the moments I least expect it that He flows the most freely. The presence of God is visible. His radiancy becomes mine and shines on the hurting hearts, the lonely hearts, the craving hearts. As I bask in the refreshing streams of the Living Water, Jesus Christ, lasting peace and spiritual refreshment emanate. In sincere faith and knowledge of my full cleansing in Him, I cry, "Jan, do not be troubled and do not be afraid. Jesus has overcome the world. You have victory in Him."

Chapter 6

THE APPLE OF HIS EYE -A GARDENER'S DELIGHT

The luscious, shiny apples filled the bowl. Everyone eyed the tempting fruit. The women verbalized their hunger. Finally, the leader passed the bowl around the circle. Instructing each woman to take an apple, she, however, had one stipulation - it could not be eaten.

Although disappointment reigned, each woman followed the instructions. Harboring one of the ripe, red glories in their hands, the leader then continued. "Now I want you to go to a secluded area and, for the next fifteen minutes, examine this apple carefully. Look at its warts, moles, bumps, coloring, stem, etc. At the end of the fifteen minutes, I will call you back to this spot to continue the test."

Giddy and confused, the women separated - all to their own area of privacy. Each examined, touched, and explored the apple as designated. Some reacted with embarrassment at the thought of getting to know this simple object. Others complied with fervor and intensity as they proceeded to acquaint themselves with "their new-found friend". Yet, all completed their assignment and returned with giggles at the appointed time.

Much to the shock and dismay of all present, the leader again passed the bowl, demanding that each place her apple back. Then, before setting the bowl of apples aside, she mixed them all up so that none nestled in the same location. Disgruntled and confused, the women wondered what she had in mind.

Nothing further was said about the apples until about an hour later. In the interim, other leaders conducted a Bible study, speaking of the uniqueness and precious qualities each person possessed. As God spoke to their hearts about His loving desire for them in His life, a light bulb began to click in the heads of a few women. Did the apple correlate with this study?

As they soon learned, the leader again took the bowl of apples and placed them before the eyes of the women. The leader then said, "Now I want you to pick out the apple you examined, explored, and held."

As the bowl flowed around the circle, an interesting phenomenon occurred. Amidst shocked responses and gasps and awes, each woman - one-by-one - claimed the apple she had previously studied. Not one claimed another's apple. Not one lacked the ability to see and accept their chosen, tasty fruit. It's characteristics had become all too familiar. As each glistening fruit rested in the hand of its rightful owner, the women prided themselves in "knowing" their respective apples. Could it be possible that God knows us with the same intimacy?

YOU ARE HAND-PICKED

"Praise be to the God and Father of our Lord Jesus Christ, who has blessed us in the Heavenly realms with every spiritual blessing in Christ. For he chose us in him before the creation of the world to be holy and blameless in his sight. In love he predestined us to be adopted as his sons through Jesus Christ in accordance with his pleasure and will - to the praise of his glorious grace, which he has freely given us in the One he loves. In him we have redemption through his blood, the forgiveness of sins, in accordance with the riches of God's grace, that he lavished on us with all wisdom and understanding. (Eph. 1:3-8)

The ripe and juicy apples on the tree waited expectantly. Their skin, though dull in color, would soon shine from polishing. As the gardener drew close, the apples sighed with expectation. Each knew the touch of his tender hand, for this gardener spent days and hours shielding it, caring for it and guarding it from harm. They loved the gardener and always responded with gratefulness to the master's touch.

While the scenario is farfetched, it provides an apt example of our relationship to the Guardian and Caretaker of our lives. As the gardener meticulously chose, selected, and cared for the apples, so God shields, cares for, and guards us as the apple of His eye. (Deut. 32:9,10)   Viewing us through eyes of love, He cherishes the responsibility for our upbringing, our care taking, our hand-picking. As the apple on the tree is helpless, He understands our helplessness and desires that we rest in Him in the process.

Eph. 1:3-8 illustrates this beautifully. We discover that we are not only hand- picked, but fed, nourished, and filled with the juicy meat of His power, love and grace. It is in Him that we become fulfilled and productive. As we draw closer to Him, we discover and acknowledge our own ineffectiveness and inability to be productive without Him. The need for His tender touch pervades our lives and we sigh in anticipation and expectation when seeking His presence.

God promises to bless "us in the Heavenly realms with every spiritual blessing in Christ." Understanding that the "Heavenly realms" houses "spiritual blessings", not material, we seek the glory of Jesus by searching His word and resting in Him and His promises. Pondering on His cross we see the ultimate goodness that the Holy One can instill on us - forgiving love, mercy, and grace. Through the gentle moving of His Spirit, we discover an inheritance that turns our eyes Heavenward, awarding us with all the spiritual blessings of Heaven itself. Fixing our eyes on Jesus, we grow into a loving, nurturing relationship that lasts into eternity.

"For he chose us in him before the creation of the world to be holy and blameless in His sight." Oh, the fullness of His love for us! He knew of us before the first word of creation flowed from His mouth. Planned in His infinite mind before the world began, He ordained that we would become His, to be loved and to love in return. Looking beyond the blood-stained cross of His Son, Jesus Christ, the Father prearranged our life with Him, first on earth, then into eternity. We are holy and blameless, not because we did anything to deserve it, but because He passed it on to us by that cross. No one else could achieve it - only the Resurrected Christ.

He determined before time that those whom He made alive, He would adopt as sons and daughters "through Jesus Christ in accordance with his pleasure and will." He loves us so much that our planned adoption existed long before we were even a twinkle in our mother's eye. We are legally adopted - and for what? For His pleasure and will. He enjoys our company. The companionship and fellowship of His beloved ones harbors an intense joy when we are present and a gnawing ache when absent. Christ, in His glory, gave His all that we might share this relationship with Him. And the amazing thing - it's freely given to us. It's ours, simply by faith and acceptance. What excitement reigns when the "apple of His eye" responds to all He has to offer!

But God's grace doesn't end there. "In him we have redemption through his blood, the forgiveness of sins, in accordance with the riches of God's grace that he lavished on us with all wisdom and understanding." Not only do we share the wonders of His kingdom, wallow in His goodness and emerge as precious, He grants to us the ultimate - redemption and forgiveness. Lavishing us with His wisdom and understanding, our eyes open to His impact in our lives. No longer seen as unacceptable, we sigh with relief at the amazing love and power available to us through Him. Unfathomable gratitude follows.

Women of faith! God hand-picked you. He adopted you. In Christ, you are holy and blameless, endowed with all the spiritual blessings of the Heavenlies. Do you believe it? Do you claim it? "In him", in Christ Jesus, you are fully redeemed. All your sins, past and present, stand before Him canceled. While Satan desires that you refuse Christ's sacrifice, denial crushes the very fulfillment and purpose of the cross. Promises of Scripture uphold that truth. Believe His word. Claim it. Resist Satan. He will flee.

"For as high as the Heavens are above the earth, so great is his love for those who fear him; as far as the east is from the west, so far has he removed our transgressions from us." (Ps. 103:11.12) "God made him (Jesus) who had no sin to be sin for us, so that in him we might become the righteousness of God." (2 Cor. 5:21) "Therefore, brothers, since we have confidence to enter the Most Holy Place by the blood of Jesus, by a new and living way opened for us through the curtain, that is, his body, and since we have a great priest over the house of God, let us draw near to God with a sincere heart in full assurance of faith, having our hearts sprinkled to cleanse us from a guilty conscience and having our bodies washed with pure water. Let us hold unswervingly to the hope we profess, for he who promised if faithful." (Hebrews 10:19-23)

LAVISHED, WE RESPOND

Lavished with all the riches of God's grace, polished by the Caretaker in the midst of the rainstorms, wind and freezing conditions (trials), nourished by the richest of fertilizers (God's wisdom and understanding through His Word), the chosen children respond by yielding the best of fruit. In Him, the response for the Heavenly blessings motivates us to serve, to care, to forgive, to love. While not always easy on our own, in Him it becomes possible. The sweet juices of His goodness pour out to others through us as we learn to yield to His generous care taking and to trust His promises offered in Scripture. For as John says, "We know that we have come to know him if we obey his commands. The man who says, 'I know him,' but does not do what he commands is a liar, and the truth is not in him. But if anyone obeys his word, God's love is truly made complete in him. This is how we know we are in him: Whoever claims to live in him must walk as Jesus did." (1 John 2:3-6, italics mine)

Living the fruitful, abundant, obedient life does not come easy. Often the first steps needed to generate a committed life for Christ in words and actions grind at our very being and resistance prevails. The forward, positive movement to care for "in spite of", to love "even though" and to forgive "when" dominates our thinking and the battle for obedience is lost even before it begins. Until we understand that receiving God's strength involves trust and that His fruits of love, joy, peace and patience cannot surface without first yielding ourselves to Him and taking the first steps toward obedience as an act of our own will.

Abiding in Him through His word remains a priority. Humanly we cannot generate the needed attributes or attitudes of divine grace to grant to others without first being connected to the source or the vine, Jesus Christ. "I am the true vine, and my Father is the gardener. He cuts off every branch in me that bears no fruit, while every branch that does bear fruit he prunes so that it will be even more fruitful...Remain in me, and I will remain in you. No branch can bear fruit by itself; it must remain in the vine. Neither can you bear fruit unless you remain in me. I am the vine; you are the branches. If a man remains in me and I in him, he will bear much fruit; apart from me you do nothing...If you remain in me and my words remain in you ask whatever you wish, and it will be given you. This is to my Father's glory, that you bear much fruit, showing yourselves to be my disciples. As the Father has loved me, so I have loved you. Now remain in my love. If you obey my commands, you will remain in my love, just as I have obeyed my Father's commands and remain in his love. I have told you this so that my joy may be in you and that your joy may be complete." (John 15:1-2,4-5,7-11, italics mine)

Past experiences and relationships bring to remembrance individuals who harbored anger for a loved one, a family member, or a close friend. Forgiveness remained out of the question. No steps of reconciliation were ever attempted.

Marriages, where spouses desire "their own rights" or "want their own freedom," end in divorce simply because steps toward a selfless sacrifice fail to exist.

Children run away, display rebellion, and cause heartbreak. Yet hurt and angry parents refuse to respond when a possibility of reconciliation occurs.

Injuries to body and spirit, injuries from drunk drivers, alcoholic and abusive parents, murderers, rapists - create deep-seeded anger and bitterness. Rather than using it as an opportunity to practice Christ's forgiveness and allow healing to take place, we wallow in self-pity and use it as an excuse for negative behaviors. Yet, until a surrender of the past rests in His hands, we will walk in pain and darkness the rest of our lives. Straining ahead to reach His goal, we discover peace, and a forgiving spirit pervades. That first step depends on us. He will then follow with His strength and grace, one step at a time.

You may be saying, "Well, I've never had those things happen to me. I don't have a problem." But I ask, "What about those little things your husband, or your boss, or your children do that irritate you and that you often 'remind' them of? How do you react when things don't happen the way you want? What happens when you are hurt by another family member and you just can't seem to let it go?" These are simpler events but carry the same weight in God's eyes. Obedience says, "Forgive". Love says, "Don't bear a record of wrongs." Trust says, "Cast your cares on Christ and let Him handle the situation."

In all these things, stay connected to the Vine. As the Gardener prunes and polishes, the Vine nourishes and sustains. Remember - as the "apple of His eye", we produce fruit, juicy and beautiful in His eyes, because we reflect all of the qualities of the Savior, the person Jesus Christ.

Chapter 7

AT HIS RIGHT HAND -ETERNAL PLEASURE

The children and I loved walking through the malls, observing all the hub-bub, gaily lit stores, and new trends. The exuberance and unrestrained joy of the children always touched my heart and refreshed me. While money was tight, they never complained about these evenings as they concluded with a special treat of their choice.

On one such evening, I happened to glance in a store window for a brief period of time. Looking forward again, I smiled, knowing all four of my children would be bouncing and laughing in front of me. Suddenly, I realized that only three children were visible. In horror, I cried, "Trina, Jeremy's missing!"

Stopping abruptly, the other three children spun around, then stared at me with puzzled looks. After a moment of silence, Trina spoke, "Mom, you're holding his hand."Looking down into the big blue eyes of five-year-old Jeremy, also bewildered, I broke out in uproarious laughter followed by the giggles of my four children. So deeply engrossed in the joy of the evening, I had forgotten that Jeremy had previously slipped his little hand in mine. "How could I forget?" I thought. "How could I forget someone so important?"

Being a teacher awards me with one of the greatest pleasures of life - holding the little hands of children. Every time a small hand slips into mine, I am reminded of God's generosity. He abundantly provides me with His little ones to love, to serve, and with whom to pass on His love. Receptive hearts and enthusiastic spirits rest within, and the squeeze of that little hand allows me the freedom of never forgetting His own tender, gentle love for me. While I may humanly forget the hand I am holding, He never will. In fact, He is so intent on remembering us that He engraved, or deeply cut, our name in the palm of His own hand. (Is. 49:16) Committing Himself to us and our best interest, He observes those names constantly. Not a minute goes by that He does not think about us or cry with us or laugh with us.

One of the most comforting passages in Scripture regarding His guidance and presence can be found in Psalm 139. "Where can I go from your Spirit? Where can I flee from your presence? If I go up to the Heavens, you are there; If I make my bed in the depths, you are there. If I rise on the wings of the dawn, if I settle on the far side of the sea, even there your hand will guide me, your right hand will hold me fast." (vs. 7-10)

After the death of my first husband, I encountered months of despair, loneliness and unending fears. As nights dragged, I often used a simple means of comfort. Resting my right hand over the side of the bed, I envisioned Jesus sitting in the chair next to me with His right hand securely holding mine. Feeling safe, I rested easier. Although the pain and grief lasted several years, the tenderness experienced through those shared times with Him will last a lifetime. I realize now that, although He did not immediately remove the experience, He did sustain and strengthen me through the valley. His right hand did guide me. It held me fast.

I recall a story of a young child walking on an icy sidewalk with his father. At first the young child, secure in his own abilities, wanted to walk without the aid of his father. Suddenly, he slipped and fell and hurt his arm. Struggling again to go it alone, he slipped again, this time injuring his leg. Looking at his daddy, he said, "Maybe I'll just hold onto your finger." With that they walked a little further. Before long, the child slipped again, releasing his hold from his father's finger. Landing promptly on his already sore arm, he decided to grab hold of his father hand. Sure that now he could tackle any icy spot, he confidently risked the treacherous terrain. Hitting again another icy spot, he lost hold of the father's hand and fell with a crash, bumping his head. Finally, in desperation, he tearfully looked at the big hand reaching out to him and said, "Daddy, I think I'll let you hold my hand!" With that, they both tackled the slippery sidewalk and moved on safely to home.

All too often in our lives, we are like that little boy. Thinking we are secure in our own persons to tackle the icy roads of life, we move onward depending on our own strength. As each icy spot becomes more treacherous and difficult, we decide we need God's help a little more. Eventually, we might even reach a time when we commit our lives enough to Him that we grab hold of His might and strength in our lives. But it isn't until the big bumps, the devastating, you-can't go-it-alone bumps, that we finally cry out and say, "Daddy, please take my hand and lead me home." The ice is still there. The opportunity to fall doesn't go away. But because He holds our hand, the ability to step beyond the hard crashes and move homeward becomes a reality.

THE WORD "I"

"'You are my servant, I have chosen you and not cast you off'; fear not, for I am with you, be not dismayed, for I am your God; I will strengthen you, I will help you, I will uphold you with my victorious right hand." (Is. 41:9,10, RSV)

Notice the frequency of the word "I" used in the preceding passage. The only thing we are told to do is to "fear not". The remainder of the verbs are preceded by God using the word "I". It is God who has chosen us. It is God who will not cast us off. He will strengthen, help, and uphold us. He knows our human frame and provides the might, strength, and power through His victorious right hand to sustain us as we walk, or drag, or saunter through this earthly life. No matter how low our opinion of ourselves, or the guilt under which we wallow, or the strain under which we live, He loves us. He forgives us. He lifts us up. But that can only be done by acknowledging our complete dependency on Him. And that's an extremely difficult task for many - especially strong-willed, independent people. Yet until we rest in His goodness and allow His Spirit to grip our lives with the presence of Jesus, we will never be totally free.

It is truly sad that many Christians today are content with a mediocre relationship with God. An abundance of eternal pleasures are available. "I have set the Lord always before me. Because he is at my right hand, I will not be shaken...You have made known to me the path of life; you will fill me with joy in your presence, with eternal pleasures at your right hand." (Ps. 16:8.11)

Some are content with a Sunday morning mentality (mostly to appease the conscience or acquire His favor). Others may desire the material over the deep spiritual pleasures of the soul. While promises of joy, confidence, a direction in life, contentment, guidance, wisdom - things of lasting value - are available at His right hand, all too many refuse these gifts from His generous hand because the fear of "giving up too much" looms before them. Yet, when eyes focus on the shed blood of Jesus and the nail-scarred hands engraved for us, the inner release of this earth slowly dissipates and the eternal overwhelms. The more we accept His Spirit's grip on us, the freer we become. Our self-esteem rises, not because we are worthy, but because His covering of love presents us before the Father as cleansed, holy, and pure. Facing the Father at the throne of grace, we are washed, renewed, and revived - to love, to serve and to praise. "Therefore, there is now no condemnation for those who are in Christ Jesus." (Rom. 8:1) "How much more, then will the blood of Christ, who through the eternal Spirit offered himself unblemished to God, cleanse our consciences from acts that lead to death, so that we may serve the living God!" (Heb. 9:14)

THE RIGHT HAND OF FELLOWSHIP

In many churches, a time is set aside to greet one another with the right hand of fellowship. As eyes meet, smiles radiate, and words of joy and comfort present themselves, a warmth envelopes the congregations. The knowledge of being part of the body of Christ assures those present of the welcoming Spirit's presence. With the right hand of fellowship, then, comes the warmth and support offered freely from another.

The Father also desires our fellowship. His right hand constantly reaches out to us in love. As we say, "Too busy" or "Not now", His loving hand stretches even further. His heart aches and grieves for those He loves - for those who refuse to grasp the hand that holds the Son's scars of sacrifice. Warmth and support, courage and strength, leadership and authority flow from that tender hand of mercy, yet are often rejected.

David, the psalm writer, understood God's fellowship and yearned for the empowerment warranted through the acceptance of it. "My soul clings to you; your right hand upholds me." (Ps. 63:8) "Your hand is strong, your right hand exalted. Righteousness and justice are the foundation of your throne; love and faithfulness go before you." (Ps. 89:13,14) "Shouts of joy and victory resound in the tents of the righteous: 'The Lord's right hand has done mighty things! The Lord's right hand is lifted high; the Lord's right hand has done mighty things!'" (Ps. 118:15,16)

Often we wonder why we feel unfulfilled. Emptiness, boredom, and frustrations abound. The humdrum overwhelms and we turn to others, to the material, to outward sources (soap operas, alcohol, drugs), and even to the New Age philosophy to discover comfort. We assume it's our husband's fault or the fault of our children. And even if we can't locate someone to "blame", we assume something is wrong with us. Yet the answer is only a fingertip away.

I can relate. I do understand. After the birth of our fourth child, I experienced an emptiness I couldn't relate to. I loved all my children and found caring for them special. Yet something snapped, causing what I call "burn-out". The diapers (dear ladies, that was before disposables), the bottles, the laundry, the cooking, the cleaning, bored me to tears. Disappearing into fantasy through the soaps became my greatest excitement. I couldn't wait for one couple to separate and another to get together. I showed frustration with the evil wench who stirred up the waters and couldn't wait for revenge. The house became cluttered and dirty (not my normal mode). Although I cared well for the children, sometimes they had to sit on my lap during an episode so as not to miss the days happening.   My world revolved around fantasy. I often yearned for the excitement and romance, feeling trapped in my own circumstances.

Suddenly one day, I looked at my precious fourteen-month-old son, Jeremy and cried. I realized that the waste I currently made of my life had to change. I loved my children and, although worn with the responsibilities and boredom, I understood that God blessed me richly through them. It seemed as if scales fell from my eyes when the TV soap came into view. Therein rested the true emptiness. The meaningless and uncommitted love, the lack of reality, the lifestyles they lived, all protruded as stark reminders that theirs was not truly the direction I desired to live. On my knees, I prayed, "Abba, Daddy, please bring meaning in my life again. Give me the desire to give up the hold these shows have on me and help me regain a spiritual sense of balance and love. I can't do it without you. Amen."

In the days that followed, with children playing and resting and snuggling next to me, I chose to read Scriptures rather than wallow in the sordid lives of TV tragedies. I journaled my thoughts, my emotions, my desires, opening myself to His leading and guidance.

Within two weeks, a part-time job opening in a Christian organization surfaced. A neighbor offered to baby-sit at a reasonable rate. My few absences, set at my own convenience, awarded a small income and gave me a focus on someone other than myself. Having the freedom to dress-up occasionally and the respite with adults brought new dreams, new hopes and new direction in my life. Two years later, I received a job as a preschool teacher at a school which Jeremy could attend. Within the next year, I returned to college part-time and renewed my teaching certification. At the end of two years, my first husband Tom died from a rare liver disorder and doors were opened to return to teaching full-time with the additional blessing that all four children attend the same school.

God's goodness and over-flowing right hand merely waited for me to allow Him to gently accept His tender hold. Upon doing so, His leading opened doors, relieved me of the doldrums, and brought excitement and enthusiasm back into my life.

As years have passed, I now realize that His outpouring, generous hand never ceases to amaze me. But the hardest lesson for me to learn was that of yielding. Too stubborn to let His grasp hold tightly, I wanted to go it alone - thus controlling my own life. As I accepted His loving control, prayed for courage to trust Him, and slipped my hand into His, I saw His mighty strength fill me to overflowing with joy as only He can do. With Him walking at my side, my icy sidewalks may bruise me but will never break me. He is my support, my strength, and my love. He is all I need.

Chapter 8

GOD'S EVERLASTING ARMS -REDEMPTION THROUGH SACRIFICE

Gazing at a picture of Jesus holding a small, dark-headed boy reminded me of the loving father and husband I inherited for a total of seventeen years. Often during the children's sermons given in church, he lovingly cradled children in his arms in full view of the congregation. Never did one cry. Never did one ask to be put down. The comfort found while resting in their minister's arms pacified them momentarily. Often perceived by them as "Jesus" with his long-flowing white robe, they appeared secure in his presence.

That same picture settled in my mind during Tom's prolonged illness and after his eventual death. As Tom often held children during his sermon illustrations, I imagined him now being the recipient of Jesus' embrace. Having succumbed to many tests and surgeries over a two year period, while racked with intense pain, I know those same arms carried him home to his Heavenly Father.

"See, the Sovereign Lord comes with power, and his arm rules for him...He tends his flock like a shepherd: He gathers the lambs in his arms and carries them close to his heart; he gently leads those that have young." (Is. 40:10,11)

The beautiful imagery of Jesus, the Good Shepherd, hovering over his sheep, caring for them, tending for their daily physical and spiritual needs paints a picture of awesome tenderness between those for whom He died and the Caretaker. Whether weak, sorrowing, vibrant, on the mountain-tops, new in the faith, wandering aimlessly through life, or maybe even separated temporarily from Him through a downhill lifestyle, He desires to cuddle us near His heart. A love beyond comprehension rests in that heart. Nothing we do can change that. "And I pray that you, being rooted and established in love, may have power, together with all the saints, to grasp how wide and long and high and deep is the love of Christ, and to know this love that surpasses knowledge - that you may be filled to the measure of all the fullness of God." (Eph. 3:17-19)

Often when I speak to Bible classes or groups, I express my deep desire to literally open my love-laden heart to them. I yearn to pour some of His love into their hearts that they may experience for themselves the precious, awesome Lord I know. I ache deeply inside for everyone to know Him as I do - to love Him as I do. While that love is a gift available to all for the asking, I am saddened to report that it is not desired by all.

Yet for many we find ourselves at a point in our own lives where the inner void for Him is so intense that we spiritually cry out in despair and open our broken hearts to Him. Admitting our helplessness and desire to draw closer to Him, we claim the verse, "Ask and it will be given to you; seek and you will find; knock and the door will be opened to you. For everyone who asks receives; he who seeks finds; and to him who knocks, the door will be opened." (Matt. 7:7,8)

In our search for Him, we discover a God who desires to carry us, console us, and cherish us. As we grow in our understanding of the Good Shepherd who laid down His life for us, we are overcome with the fullness of joy that is found only in Him. Hugging us tightly, He carries us through life, promising to never leave us or forsake us. Even when the road takes dark turns and the valleys seem excruciating, He is there, softening the burden, strengthening the heart. It isn't until the pain is past that we see His radiancy and love, for it now fills us and enables us to help carry others. That is His greatest legacy!

LISTEN TO HIS VOICE

"My sheep listen to my voice; I know them and they follow me. I give them eternal life, and they shall never perish; no one can snatch them out of my hand.. My Father, who has given them to me, is greater than all; no one can snatch them out of my Father's hand. I and the Father are one." (John 10:27-29)

Secure in His arms, heeding His calling voice, we rest in the assurance that no one and nothing can ever remove us from our Source of eternal love. We personally can reject it but it cannot happen against our will and certainly is never His will.

Often circumstances in life leave us wondering why cruelty, dishonesty, pain, suffering, and despair abound. But even when things don't make sense, we must claim His promises of strength and acknowledge our trust in Him, one day at a time - sometimes one moment at a time. He assures us of His covering even though it may appear absent for a time. The eternal purposes of God are past understanding and we must cling to His ever-present wisdom. Trust in the midst of difficulties and hardships beckons us, for He says, "Trust in the Lord with all you heart and lean not on your own understanding; In all your ways acknowledge him, and he will make your paths straight." (Prov. 3:5,6)

Even in the midst of our circumstances of life - both good and bad - we need to pray, "Help us, O God our Savior, for the glory of your name; deliver us and forgive our sins for your name's sake...May the groans of the prisoners come before you; by the strength of your arm preserve those condemned to die." (Ps. 79:9,11) While we may not be actual prisoners as the Israelites when held in Babylonian captivity, we are often held captive by our own habits, desires, and sinful life. Trapped in a state of despair and confusion and floundering in our slippery places, we yearn for release. As we turn to Him for deliverance and forgiveness, His loving, gracious arms embrace us and pull us out of the depths to be restored into the light of His presence.

Surrendering to Him, we gain freedom - freedom found only in Christ - and a rescue. In the process, we realize that our reliance on self must not rest in our own accomplishments, but rather in the shed blood of Jesus Christ. He and He alone purified and cleansed us and restored us to the Father's love. It has already been accomplished. We can add nothing to it. Our Heavenly goal now is to glorify His holy name and to do His Father's will. "Save your people and bless your inheritance; be their shepherd and carry them forever." (Ps. 28:9)

THE LOVING ARMS OF REDEMPTION

The story is told of a drawbridge operator who enjoyed his occupation immensely. One of his favorite events occurred when his young son joined him and watched the careful and methodical workings of lowering and raising the bridge as trains approached and passed by. The timing had to be just perfect. Nothing dared be eliminated or altered. The lives of everyone on the train rested in the father's hands.

On one such occasion, after hearing the train whistle, the young son decided to go outside to watch the huge gears turn as the bridge went down. He was fascinated by its workings and often spent hours watching it. As the train neared, the father called the son inside in order to remove the young boy from danger. Unfortunately the son did not come. Again, he called and heard a faint cry, "Daddy, my arms are caught." The young lad, this day, decided to play among the gears and suddenly found himself wedged between them. The father found himself trapped in a grueling dilemma. Because of the timing, he knew he needed to begin operating the bridge or the train full of people would fall to their death. Yet if he began the process, his son would be crushed to death in the turning of the gears. No time remained. A decision, however difficult, needed to be made. Finally, his hand raised to begin pushing the buttons on the drawbridge. As the bridge went down, the father began to hear the screams of his son. Yet there was nothing he could do. He must stay there and desert his son or the lives of hundreds would be lost. As the bridge closed and the train whizzed by, the father looked at the happy, excited faces of those on the train, totally oblivious to the price that had just been paid to save their lives. But deep in the father's heart, the remembrance of his son's screams crushed his very heart and soul. Would they ever know? Would they ever understand?

Our loving Father in Heaven asks those same questions of us, for on one black Friday, His Son paid a price beyond human comprehension. While the Father listened to His cries of physical pain and hellish torment, most were oblivious to the intensity of the sacrifice He made. Few also understood the heart of a Father that would relinquish His own Son to such torture for the sake of millions. Turning His back, the Father made a choice - the eternal reward of many for the death of His One. Would they ever know? Would they ever understand?

As the arms of the Father granted salvation through the loving arms of Jesus, so today those arms still stretch out to us, calling us back. As He said to the people of Israel, so He says to us, "'...I will redeem you with an outstretched arm and with mighty acts of judgment. I will take you as my own people, and I will be your God.'" (Ex. 6:6,7)

Never doubt your self-worth. Resting in the powerful, expressive action of Jesus Christ, He visually and completely rescued us from our life of sin, granting us total freedom in Him. Salvation is secure. Both the Father and the Son resolutely shouted then and now, " I love you. The proof rests in the cross and in resurrection. Please believe and be saved."

But where does that leave me today? So I'm saved for the future - how can that help me now?

Be assured that the crushing of bones on the cross, the cruel torment of hell for the sins of all, the tender love of the Son, is available today. By drawing into His presence through prayer, Bible study, and constant fellowship with the Victor over sin, eternal life is ours today. His peace, His goodness and His power pour into us through His Spirit. Yielding to Him and surrendering to His will brings freedom, a freedom only known in Him. Our burdens tumble onto His back. Our self-esteem, centered in His forgiving grace, grants us new perspective and hope. The crushed arms cradle us and comfort us forever. The victory is won!

"Sing to the Lord a new song, for he has done marvelous things; his right hand and his holy arm have worked salvation for him." (Ps. 98:1)

"Shout for joy to the Lord, all the earth. Worship the Lord with gladness; come before him with joyful songs. Know that the Lord is God. It is he who made us, and we are his; we are his people, the sheep of his pasture. Enter his gates with thanksgiving and his courts with praise; give thanks to him and praise his name. For the Lord is good and his love endures forever; his faithfulness continues through all generations." (Ps. 100)

"This is how God showed his love among us: He sent his one and only Son into the world that we might live through him. This is love: not that we loved God, but that he loved us and sent his Son as an atoning sacrifice for our sins." (1 John 4:9,10)

Chapter 9

THE SHADOW OF YOUR WINGS -SOARING TO THE HEIGHTS

"Dear God, where is my suitcase? I'm at wits end and need a vacation. Today, the two boys dumped half the water from the commode onto the bathroom floor. The girls had a spitting contest in bed. Jeremy destroyed a full tube of new lipstick by smearing it over his entire face. Dinner burned. The dishwasher broke. I cut my finger while slicing a lemon. It's the first day of my monthly, with cramps coming out of my yazoo. Tom called to say he is staying at the conference an extra day and to make matters worse, the tornado siren went off last night and the kids and I were forced to scurry down the basement steps at 2:00a.m alone. I know 'Momma said there would be days like this', but I'm not sure I can cope. How much worse can it get?"

Hiding is a concept many mothers understand. Taking a comic book to the bathroom and locking the door helps but doesn't prevent the proverbial knock at the door with a timid voice from the other side saying, "Mommy."

Taking an afternoon nap certainly has its rewards and benefits but culminates with the ringing of the phone, followed by the crying of one or more of the children. They say there is no rest for the wicked. "Lord, I must be terribly wicked."

Or is it blessed? Think of those innocent cherubs we swoon over while sleeping. Those cuddly hugs and warm fuzzies - "Mom, look what I made for you!" "Mom, I luv you." As we mend the cuts and kiss the scrapes we see a vision of God's goodness in our own lives. Our small booboo's are touched and kissed and embraced as we see His love in their faces.

But there are days - days of desired suitcase packing, days of utter frustration, days of a genuine hankering for a time of rest. Where is my hiding place if the bathroom won't work? I often thought of building a nest under the house, coated with pillows, warm teddy bears and quiet music. But then I knew, even if I tried, I would still hear the tramping of feet above me and the quiet voices through the floorboard, "Mommy." And being the mommy I am, I'd give up my pillowed, secluded place to care for the precious, yet sometimes challenging, bundles of joy with which God blessed me. After all, they were sent to earth to do my Father's will, just as I was. I needed to care for His precious cargo. What a great and awesome responsibility He gave me!

Then they grow up - Late night dates, sneaking out after hours, "stylish" clothing, unfinished homework. "Can I have the car tonight, Mom?" "Why won't you let me spend the night with the others in a motel after the prom?" "Everyone else is doing it!" "Salad again? - I call it sticks and leaves." Oh, the bigger the kids, the bigger the challenges. Where once I was able to control the menagerie with a few minutes of simple punishment, now they succumb to days of punishment called "grounding". The only problem - who suffers the most? As they lay around with nothing to do or grump at the list of chores, Mom endures - and endures - and endures. Jumping high on a trampoline cannot come close to the jumps of joy expressed by Mother when the grounding is over as she moves on to bigger and better things.

But even then, the fun times far surpass the frustrations. Watching them dressed to kill for a prom or Christmas dance causes my heart to burst with pride. A job well done in school or at work renews the hope in life-with-teens. Activity in church, youth conferences attended, big hugs (cautiously given) - all render encouragement. Laughter over spilled milk, the dog's tricks, or silly games warm the heart.

In the order of good things, I survived. Yet I know that other moms sometimes wonder how they personally accomplish it. Some barely do. Problems with drinking, smoking, drugs, sexual promiscuity, and homosexuality cause devastation and despair. Problems that can not easily - if at all - be erased. "Where do I go now, Lord? I need a resting place. I need a place to feel warm and cozy and to be refreshed. Show me that place."

Compound these events with difficulties with spouses, parents and other siblings, work, church, and health. Days seem endless. The end seems days away. Depression overwhelms and many don't know how to overcome. Often hated is the routine life, yet others wish the routine would resurface. Nothing is predictable. Nothing is sure. Or is it?

Like a powdered-sugar coating on top of lemon bars, so my life appears sometimes. All sweetness on the surface with a bit of sour underneath. Knowing the healthy growth of my children depends on maintaining a calm exterior, God's strength allows me to remain loving, tender, and gentle. Yet at times, I wonder if I am as successful as I desire. Motherhood absorbs my every minute, even when at work. The care of sick children, the knowledge of sibling rivalries, and the concern over problems with schoolwork surface many times a day. The "sour" in me desires to surface and only with knees bent and fingers intertwined in prayer does the "sweetness" take over again.

When my father died three weeks after my husband, I wondered where I could go to escape. He had often been my sounding board when the sour lemons surfaced. The faith he shared and the love he gave always boosted me and gave me the "umph" I needed to go on. Now, both my husband and father were gone.

Candidly, I addressed my need. "Lord, who do I go to now when I feel like packing that suitcase? Where is that listening ear?" Soothing messages never ceased to follow my questions. Often it took journaling coupled with Scripture searching to discover the answer. And that answer remained constant - "I AM" all you need.

It never ceased to amaze me how often my flounderings seemed so wasted when the God of grace and love stood valiantly at the door of my heart, waiting to leap in and restore, replenish, and revitalize my spirit. So much energy wasted. So much time in communion with Him delayed. He desired for me to crawl under His wings of mercy and find comfort, but I kept trying to solve it all myself.

IN THE SHELTER OF HIS WINGS

"Hear my cry, O God; listen to my prayer. From the ends of the earth I call to you, I call as my heart grows faint; lead me to the rock that is higher than I. For you have been my refuge, a strong tower against the foe. I long to dwell in your tent forever and take refuge in the shelter of your wings." Ps. 61: 1-4

On good days, I remain content with life. Little ruffles my feathers. Other days, things only go from bad to worse. One frustration after another only creates an atmosphere where my tolerance level reaches an all time low. The opening story is a classic example. While I must admit that not all these truly happened in one day, they did all happen - and many in close proximity. These days could stand in the Hallmark Hall of Fame as my most trying days on record. Often, I desired a refuge.

In the Old Testament, God resided in a tent - the tent of meeting or tabernacle. Enthroned above the cover of the ark of testimony, between of the wings of the cherubim, He promised to dwell. (Ex. 25:22) Moses met with Him often and found a resting place.   David did the same.   They relished in His presence and found spiritual protection, comfort, and refuge in the shelter of those wings.

The concept of God's "wings" enables me to visualize the ability to soar above my worries and concerns. As He now resides in my "tent", my flawed and sometimes exhausted body, so He gives me the power to carry on. The tender relationship I experience in His presence fills my spirit with hope, encouragement and peace. Without being sheltered by His wings, I flail about.   Under those wings, His strength is promised during my weakness, no matter how intense.(2 Cor. 12:9)

Occasionally in our personal lives, we believe God should remove the pain, the frustration, the circumstances. But God's desire goes much deeper. Spiritual growth, spiritual blessings, spiritual contentment reside in His heart as hopes for us. Warmed by His Spirit, He develops a Christ-like presence. Qualities of Jesus, the fruit of the Spirit, a gentle heart, humility - all desired by the God of love, who often must allow difficulties to penetrate.

Cruelty exists. Abuse is prevalent today. How can you say God desires that for us? I don't! But God did not bring about those events. Man did. But with eternal purposes in mind, He promises inner refuge with Him. He did not release Paul from the beatings and imprisonments. David still had to hide in caves to escape Saul's fury. James was still beheaded for his faith. Job still lost all he had, including his health. Joseph was imprisoned unjustifiably. Stephen was stoned to death by leaders of the church. People are still tortured for their faith in many countries today. Why do we think we should be void of the possibility of these? I cannot imagine the mental anguish included in any of these. I am blessed not to have experienced it. But friends have. Flashbacks, fears, heartache often surfaces. Yet, I believe God can and will use it for good.

With His sheltering wings over our spiritual lives, even in the midst of the difficulty, His power and love will be revealed and healing can take place.

With David we cry out, "Hide me in the shadow of Your wings." (Ps. 17:8) Lord, in the midst of daily routines or harried circumstances; in the depth of despair and loneliness; in the absence of loved ones or caring individuals; in the agony of cruelty and abuse - grant my a hiding place in Your presence. "You are my hiding place; you will protect me from trouble and surround me with songs of deliverance." (Ps. 32:7)"

In tender love, He responds, "I will instruct you and teach you in the way you should go; I will counsel you and watch over you." (Ps. 32:8)

His love will guide our every move. He will teach us of His love and of His Son's painful sacrifice for us. As He said to Joshua before going into battle, "I will never leave you nor forsake you." (Josh. 1:5) It's a promise - claim it!

ON EAGLE'S WINGS

Above our home, flies two of the most stately birds seen today. Being close to many lakes, eagles are prevalent. I feel most privileged to be able to observe them often. They appear as symbols of strength and power and give one hope in the freedom of soaring to the heights.

The metaphor of God's protecting care as that of eagle's wings only solidifies my intense love for Him. When describing God's great love for His chosen people, Moses responds in song, "He shielded him (Jacob) and cared for him...like an eagle that stirs up its nest and hovers over its young, that spreads its wings to catch them and carries them on its pinions."

As a mother fluffs her nest, as she hovers above them as an example of flight, as she provides daily food, as she covers her young to protect them from the scorching sun and beating rain, even as she catches them on her wings when they fall, so God fusses over us. His wings become our place of refuge and safety. No matter the surroundings or the circumstances, we cannot escape God's protecting pinions (the main feathers of bird's wings). As we rest in Him in faith and commit our lives to His goodness and guidance, He will not fail us. As the eagle is instinctively attached to its young, so God is attached to us by His very nature. His grace is sufficient. His strength abundant. As we press forward, He lifts us up as on wings of eagles, leading us ever upward toward Heaven and the blessings of life in His presence. "Those who hope in the Lord will renew their strength. They will soar on wings like eagles; they will run and not grow weary, they will walk and not be faint." (Is. 40:31)

As we seek Him in prayer and meditation, He flies to our rescue, swiftly and courageously. At the exact moment of His needed divine intervention, He swoops down, picks us up and bears us on His wings. There are seeming delays, but those delays are only in our perspective. Just as the Israelites thought God's rescue from Egypt was long in coming, so He reminds them that the opposite is true. With the swiftness of an eagle, He stepped forward and prepared the way for them to march on to their promised land. "You have seen what I did to the Egyptians, and how I bore you on eagles' wings and brought you to myself." (Ex. 19:4, RSV) His rapidness in responding brought about their salvation. But the swiftness relied on His appropriate timing and need. We cannot see the overall picture - only He can, and we must rest in that assurance. "The Lord is not slow in keeping his promise, as some understand slowness. He is patient with you, not wanting anyone to perish, but everyone to come to repentance." (2 Peter 3:9)

Resting involves trust. It requires a closing of the eyes, a mind concentrated on God's attributes. Often it demands sacrifice - a sacrifice of praise. As David ached for redemption from his enemies, being pursued in the desert of Judah, he yet could sing under the shadow of His wings. "O God, you are my God, earnestly I seek you; my soul thirsts for you, my body longs for you in a dry and weary land where there is no water. I have seen you in the sanctuary and beheld your power and your glory. Because your love is better than life, my lips will glorify you. I will praise you as long as I live, and in your name I will lift up my hands...On my bed I remember you; I think of you through the watches of the night. Because you are my help, I sing in the shadow of your wings." (Ps. 63:1-4,6-7) Hunted, haunted and hated, He faced loneliness and despair. Yet He acknowledged the greatness of His God and found refuge and safety in His presence.

At night, when all seemed most frightening, David sought God's comfort. Wrapped in the very wings He observed at the sacred ark of the testimony, He could close His eyes in rest, absorbing the loving-kindness and protection that he valued more than life itself.   Nothing would penetrate those wings without the Father's consent. God's supporting wings of love would never depart. In that thought, David rested. So we too can rest. As we close our eyes in slumber, even restless slumber, our determination to focus on Heavenly things, not earthly things, can draw us under His wings. Praising, even when it hurts, requires persistence and determination. Yet, His love never fails. He will cover you with His feathers and under His wings you will find refuge. (Ps. 91:4) You are His priority and your protection is His privilege.

Even Jesus Christ Himself expressed His desire to shield with His wings those He loved. "O Jerusalem, Jerusalem, you who kill the prophets and stone those sent to you, how often I have longed to gather your children together, as a hen gathers her chicks under her wings, but you were not willing!" (Luke 13:34) The intensity of that love never ceased to be evident, even to those who hated Him. On the cross He cried, "Father, forgive them for they do not know what they are doing." (Luke 23:34)

Jesus possessed a profound depth of love that no man can understand apart from Him. Yielding to the ultimate sacrifice and punishment for our sins, he provided the greatest covering of wings supplied by God. As the gruesome load of sin overwhelmed His very being, the covering of His forgiving wings fell on us and washed us clean. Therein lies our self-esteem. Held close to His heartbeat, snuggling in the warmth of His presence, Jesus grants us free access to the Father's throne through prayer and communion. It is not dependent on who we are, but whose we are. As we crawl under the safety of His wings, we remain safe from the sun-parched land we live in. It's a place we can go to feel safe - a place to discover new strength for our forward march, one day at a time, one hour at a time, one minute at a time. Our spirits are refreshed. Our peace restored.

Chapter 10

HIS BRIDE -HOLY AND BLAMELESS IN HIS SIGHT

Tears streamed down my face as I lay in bed suffering from deep depression. The hurt I recently incurred ravaged my heart at its very core and I desired to hide under the covers, avoiding contact with anyone else in my life. "If I remain here," I thought, "no one else can hurt me. No one else can create another stabbing pain which no surgery or medicine can cure."

Suddenly, without warning, a voice inside me whispered, "Jan, get out of bed and shower."

Stunned , I wanted to resist the voice. Yet, knowing the voice did not originate from me, I climbed out of bed and walked into the bathroom to shower.

While completing the shower, I heard the gentle voice again speak. "Jan, now put on your makeup." Although the depression weighed heavily, I completed the required task, wondering if the red, puffy eyes would be visible for weeks to come.

With makeup complete, a third time the voice whispered, "Now Jan, get dressed and go to Bible study."

Knowing now that the voice speaking had to be the Spirit, I thought, "Now You're pressing your luck, Lord. But - since it's you, I will obey."

Amazingly, in the process of dressing, an astounding peace replaced the depression. Filled now with unexpected joy, I determined to face people at the Bible study, red eyes and all. To my amazement, when I took one last look in the mirror, the red eyes were gone. No trace of crying appeared on my face, for it radiated the same joy I felt inside.

A different tear rolled down my cheek as I prayed, "Thank you, Jesus. You truly are my Husband and I praise You for pulling me from the depths and filling me with joy. How can I thank You enough?"

What a tender Husband I have! His compassions never fail. They are new every morning. Great is His faithfulness. (Lam. 3:22,23)

THE MAKER IS YOUR HUSBAND

Understanding the intimate relationship my Lord desired of me as a young Christian seldom stretched beyond accepting His goodness and trusting Him in difficulties. Growing up, I encountered times of overwhelming love, gratitude for forgiveness, and an appreciation of His sovereignty. Yet a deep, abiding love for His Eternal Presence in my life, and a personal relationship with my Savior, hadn't yet surfaced.

After my first husband's death in 1983, I encountered overwhelming emotional turmoil and despair. But I gradually grew to understand that my "broken and contrite spirit" opened the doors for the drawing of my heart into His heart (Ps. 51:17) As I searched Scripture, desiring understanding of this awesome God I worshipped, I learned of a perfect Husband whose unconditional love and concern for me went far beyond human comprehension. His attributes and qualities outweighed the negatives and I fell in deep love with the Maker - my Husband, Jesus. "For your Maker is your husband - the Lord Almighty is his name - the Holy one of Israel is your Redeemer; he is called the God of all the earth." (Is. 54:5) While I agonized through the brokenness, I would never change a day of it. For in the process, I formed a marriage relationship with my Bridegroom and I learned to acknowledge and accept the honor of being called His bride.

HE GAVE HIMSELF UP FOR ME

A beautiful example of Christ as our Bridegroom is portrayed in Paul's letter to the Ephesians. While speaking to the husbands in that culture, many who were dominating, overpowering men, Paul reveals a new and exceptional type of love - one difficult to generate without His presence in their lives.

"Husbands, love your wives, just as Christ loved the church and gave himself up for her to make her holy, cleansing her by the washing with water through the word, and to present her to himself as a radiant church, without stain or wrinkle or any other blemish, but holy and blameless. In the same way, husbands ought to love their wives as their own bodies.. He who loves his wife loves himself. After all, no one ever hated his own body, but he feeds and cares for it, just as Christ does the church - for we are members of his body." (Eph. 5:25-30) Please understand at this point that I am not inserting this passage to use as gunpowder against your husband. It is critical that we, as women, understand our role in Christ from His perspective before we acknowledge and appropriately pray for our husband's role. So often in a marriage, the husband says, "Wife, submit", which often sends shudders up one's spine. Then the wife in turn cries out, "Husband, then be like Christ." My desire is that finger-pointing be eliminated, for as long as we enlarge the other spouse's inadequacies, the more dejected and rejected we feel. Our concern and focus should remain on our own ministry, our own role as wife, our own relationship in Christ. Then through His wisdom, understanding, and love, we can follow through with words, choices, and decisions pleasing to Him.

Now we return to Paul's reference to the Ephesians. I believe there are four major coverings of love presented to us as Christ's bride. Claiming these coverings during difficult times, with a spouse or without, centers our interests and desires in Him rather than upon ourselves.

SUPREME SACRIFICE

The first covering of love - He loved us and gave Himself up for us.

"Open heart - Open home" is a phrase often heard in my relationship with my husband, Duane. Believing that we need to listen to the Lord's voice in the area of hospitality, we host meals, parties, and individuals as the Lord calls. Even though it requires energy and time, much joy overpowers as the hearts of many are reached for Him.

So it is in our lives under Christ's covering of love. He has an "Open heart - Open home" philosophy. Not only did He open His heart to us with His grace and love, but He expended an enormous amount of energy and time in the process. Giving of Himself in spiritual torment and anguish on the Calvary cross, His heart cried out to us to accept the full forgiveness and new life offered. With nail scars as the mark of hospitality, His ultimate reward proved to be joy - unexplainable, ecstatic joy. "Let us fix our eyes on Jesus, the author and perfector of our faith, who for the joy set before him endured the cross, scorning its shame, and sat down at the right hand of the throne of God. Consider him who endured such opposition from sinful men, so that you will not grow weary and lose heart." (Heb. 2:2,3) The price He paid to redeem us, to free us, to renew us held far more sacrifice than any simple acts of hospitality. Yet the joy set before Him far outweighed the pain of the cross and the shame involved. His ultimate goal resulted in restoring us to a right relationship with His Father and in encouraging us to "hang in there", using Him as an example.

CLEANSED AND WASHED

Second covering of love - Cleansed by the washing with water through the word

Having made mudpies most of the afternoon, my four cherubs entered the garage looking like mudbabies themselves. Knowing their forbidden access into our home in that condition, they yelled to me in the house to be cleansed of the filthy fun in which they imbibed. Pulling the hose from around the corner of the house, I sprayed, rubbed and even scraped the mud from between their toes, their fingers and off their faces. Giggling through the process, joy remained evident for just as the mud party held wonderful memories so did the cleansing. The only difference - the mud, if not removed would have prevented the eventual, renewed celebration of re-entry into our loving abode, while the cleansing opened the doors of "home" again and the activities inside the family dwelling became accessible.

Christ gave His life "to make (His bride) holy, cleansing her by the washing with water through the word." Stepping before the cross of Christ, we have a tendency to look at our "mud"- the sin, the mistakes. Remembering, too, the "fun" generated in the process, we might even be reluctant to have it scrubbed away. In fact, many today still can't or won't allow His cleansing flood of love to erase the mudbaby existence enjoyed. Yet, Christ reaches out as our Husband, gently touching our hearts with the assurance, "I have made you holy. I have cleansed you through baptism and the washing of my words. You are mine. My Holy Spirit will generously restore you and strengthen you."

"But when the kindness and love of God our Savior appeared, he saved us, not because of righteous things we had done, but because of his mercy. He saved us through the washing of rebirth and renewal by the Holy Spirit whom he poured out on us generously through Jesus Christ our Savior, so that, having been justified by his grace, we might become heirs having the hope of eternal life." (Titus 3:4-7)

We are holy. We are blameless. We are given new birth through baptism and the Holy Spirit. And the source is the Word - that powerful, purposeful, potent Word of God. For that Word is Christ. That Word holds His very presence. "In the beginning was the Word, and the Word was with God, and the Word was God. He was with God in the beginning...The Word became flesh and made his dwelling among us. We have seen his glory, the glory of the One and only, who came from the Father, full of grace and truth." (John 1:1-2,14)

What a privilege to hear our Bridegroom say, "I love you. I see no fault in you for I have cleansed you. You are mine."

A RADIANT BRIDE

Third covering of love - A radiant bride without stain, wrinkle, or blemish.

"I sought the Lord, and he answered me; he delivered me from all my fears. Those who look to him are radiant; their faces are never covered with shame." (Ps. 34:4,5)

Going through a period of sleeplessness after Tom's death, I hit a time of emotional devastation. Grappling with fears and inner turmoil, I needed to rest in the only One I knew could pull me through. Surrendering my being totally into His hands, I begged to be pulled from the pit, but knew it could only happen one day at a time.

During the process, I realized that many days I must have looked rather haggard for one doesn't remain "sunny" in appearance with only four or less hours of sleep. Yet, I claimed the above verse day after day. Others observed as I trusted my

Bridegroom to guide me through the dark days. I cried for His tender touch and often sobbed, "Jesus, You promised that I would be radiant. You promised that my face would never be covered with shame. I believe that and I claim it in Your name. It is Your glory I desire. Help me to rest in that promise."

As the nights became less restless and the number of hours in slumber increased, my trust became more and more secure. He did not disappoint me. In fact, I became amazingly aware of His covering of forgiving love.

So many mistakes were made during that time, not only in my personal decisions but with my children, yet I knew that my face would never be covered with shame. In His eyes I existed as a bride "without stain or wrinkle or any other blemish." (Eph. 3:27) How amazing His love! I was (and still am) holy and blameless in His sight. (Eph. 3:28)

The most exciting realization occurred when I dwelled on Paul's letter to the Romans. "And we know that in all things God works for the good of those who love him, who have been called according to his purpose." (8:28) No matter my inadequacies, my wrong choices made during grief or despair, my inability to stand more firm in some areas, Jesus would use them for good. That remained true not only of me, but of the errors I made in caring and raising my children.

One such example occurred with my daughter Trina, who was twelve at the time. Tremendous responsibility rested in her hands as I returned to full-time teaching, taking on the father role and resting the mother role on her. During my time of emotional stress and sleepless nights, I needed relief from some responsibilities, forgetting that Trina already carried a heavy load.

At the dinner table one evening, I sobbed, "You kids will have to take on more responsibility. I just can't do it all any more. You are to be responsible for finding rides to your practices and games and I am asking you to help more at home." With that, I dismissed myself to the bedroom, my haven for quiet and meditation with the Lord.

For several days after that, Trina wore a mask of President Lincoln around the house. Not understanding her reasoning, I often begged her to take it off and to join the rest of us without it. She, however, refused.

It wasn't until years later that I discovered that her use of the mask was to hide the red eyes she incurred from crying. Not desiring that she add sorrow upon sorrow, she chose to hide her pain behind the mask. For her, the request came at a time of her own depression and grief, yet I held too many deep concerns of my own to grasp the loss she incurred. Already burdened with so much, how could I ask her to do more?

As time passed, much healing replaced the open wounds. Yet burdened for a time by my lack of discernment, I despaired over the needless pain I created. Yet again I had to say, "Dear Jesus, do not let my face be covered with shame. Let them now see that in You, I am without wrinkle or blemish. I did the best I could and I must believe that even my mistakes will be used for Trina's good and Your glory. In that thought, I find peace."

So often we carry burdens far to heavy for us. We forget that the Sacrificial Lamb, our Bridegroom, yearns to carry that burden for us. He desires that we take comfort in knowing we did the best we could and that even our mistakes and flaws can be used for good when rested in His almighty hands.

"No, in all these things we are more than conquerors through him who loved us. For I am convinced that neither death nor life, neither angels nor demons, neither the present nor the future, nor any powers, neither height nor depth, nor anything else in all creation, will be able to separate us from the love of God that is in Christ Jesus our Lord." (Rom. 8:37-39)

THE ABUNDANT PROVIDER

Fourth covering of love - He feeds and cares for us

Certain of my love for my son, I desired his best. Earlier in the day he called, sharing news of a different job that paid better and would allow him to pay more of his college expenses. The only glitch seen in my eyes was the need to work forty hours the first six weeks. While Christmas break neared an end, I wondered how he could work forty hours and still carry a full load at school. Proud of him for the wonderful news, the "what-ifs" still hung over my head.

Awakening with a sweat during the night, I caught myself in a stew over this dilemma. The thought whirred around in my brain, causing shoulders to tense up and a headache to surface.

Accepting God's loving control in my life, I began quoting promises from Scripture. "God works for the good of those who love him." (Rom. 8:28) "For you are his workmanship created in Christ Jesus." (Eph. 2:10) "'I know the plans I have for you,' declares the Lord, 'plans to prosper you and not to harm you, plans to give you hope and a future.'" (Jer. 29:11)

Suddenly, while focusing on His word, a sound from the back porch startled me. A music box began playing "Away in a Manger." Realizing it to be the location of Duane's newly constructed music boxes, I could not help but smile and praise God. No one started the music. It evolved on its own from being wound too tightly. Yet, the significance of its timing created intense joy within.

As I again claimed those verses, not only for me but also for Jeremy, I knew the fulfillment of each rested in Christ and His love for both of us. Promising to trust that child in the manger, I thanked Him for the strength to accept His goodness for Jeremy. The reality - he had a great job. Fact - he was excited about the job. The power and potential strength for him would come - one day at a time.

Our Bridegroom awaits our call. He yearns to provide, to care for, and to supply all our needs. The only thing He asks is that we trust Him and that we seek His face. "Trust in the Lord with all your heart and lean not on your own understanding; in all your ways acknowledge him, and he will make your paths straight." (Pr. 3:5,6) "But seek first his kingdom and his righteousness and all these things will be given to you as well. Therefore do not worry about tomorrow, for tomorrow will worry about itself. Each day has enough trouble of its own." (Matt. 6:33,34)

The Eternal Provider of good remains available every day - one day at a time. Even when others fail us, He stands ready to fill the void. Even when our spouse, our children or our parents can't be all we want them to be, Christ Jesus says, "I am all you need. Trust Me." His mercies never end. His compassions never fail. His love abounds. Trust Him.

Chapter 11

FEET OF A DEER -CLIMB THE MOUNTAINS TO SERVE IN THE VALLEYS

As I near the end of this book, my heart aches. So much love floods my spirit and I deeply desire to pour into each of you the very essence of this overwhelming joy. Nothing in my life compares. No other creates a similar peace and comfort. I can't help but ask, "What more can I say, Lord? How can I help them understand this Heavenly ecstasy I experience in Your presence? What can I do to share it more and live it more fully? Guide me, Lord. Intervene as I try to help them see even a small window of Heaven through my words, inspired by You and moved through You."

Many times my quiet moments in the middle of the night end in unexpected touches of His love and power. Words cannot fully express this experience. His presence within me overflows and slumber is far from desired, as I fear the tender touches of His love will fade. I believe I am experiencing the joys of Heaven itself and nothing matters except my moments with Him. I wallow in unspeakable joy and spend many moments offering praise to the Father, Son and Spirit.

Often from my mouth floods the verses in Habakkuk 3:17-19: "Though the fig tree does not bud and there are no grapes on the vines, though the olive crop fails and the fields produce no food, though there are no sheep in the pen and no cattle in the stalls, yet I will rejoice in the Lord, I will be joyful in God my Savior. The Sovereign Lord is my strength; he makes my feet like the feet of a deer, he enables me to go on the heights."

There is no limit to comprehending the height, the depth, the width, or the length of His love. I recall the story of a man who encountered a near-death experience. When asked,

"What was it like?", he responded, "If you can remember the highest point of ecstasy ever experienced in your life, it does not even come close to the Heavenly experience." In Him, I find a love far beyond my expectations.

Having touched Him and reached another mountain peak, I cherish the moment but soon discover I ache for more. Remaining close to Him and spending time in His presence is coveted and earnestly sought after. Inner peace and a glowing radiance exist day after day, whether enduring difficult circumstances or experiencing times of elation and joy. His goodness far outweighs any other events in my life.

In my inner being, I yearn to become more like Christ, even when the polishing, the chiseling, the strong rivers, and the rush of mighty wings seem too fast, too harsh and too powerful. I trust His grace to shield, protect and restore. My confidence rests in the Lord of love whom I have grown to love deeply.

THE SOVEREIGN LORD IS MY STRENGTH

The powder covered the floor. Children glided across it. Adults danced over it. A rough, sticky surface became a slick surface on which many shared joy, laughter, and hours of fun. What a difference that powder made! But when the powder was removed, the rough, sticky surface emerged again. It proved only temporary. It's fun, short-lived.

So it is in our lives. We take the material, the possessions, the people, the adrenaline-highs, the danger, the alcohol, the drugs, the sex and use it to powder the rough, sticky emptiness within us, hoping to enjoy just a few hours of joy, laughter, and fun. Yet, when it ends or wears off, the old crusty, sticky hurts and emptiness return. It was only temporary. Reality returns and so does the monotony and humdrum activities of life. Another high has to be planned. Another risk has to be taken.

So when does it all end. Where can we find an end to the cycle?

I say, "Fill the void from the inside out. And that can only be done in Christ." Until we understand, accept, and surrender our lives totally into His hands we can never truly touch His throne. Unless we are stripped of our humanity and dependence on self, we can never spiritually gaze upon the face of Christ and see Him as He communes with us in our spirit. It can't be explained. It can only be experienced. And it doesn't occur only once. He pours His love on us day after day, at every moment that we cry for Him to be our Guide, our Strength, and our Joy. Alone we are helpless. With Him we overcome and remain victorious.

HE MAKES MY FEET LIKE THE FEET OF A DEER

The craggy peaks jutted ominously. Too dangerous, too impossible, we stumble backward rather than stepping forward, forgetting to cling to the promise that He will get us to the top.

When feeble cries to the Maker finally pass our lips, we discover a step we hadn't noticed. Our feet, though thick and swollen from the mountainous climb, seem to find security on that step. Looking upward, we again discover another step and our feet become even more sure. Our dependence is no longer on self but on the One who guides our footsteps ever onward - ever upward. Slowly, step-by-step, our goal of reaching the top with His wisdom and guidance surfaces as reality.

Looking down, we now discover a major change in our ability to climb. Our feet, once swollen and cut from the painful rocks, now appear healed, swift-looking, and cloven. In the process of our climb, He changed us. The ability, the strength, and the path rested in Him, not in our own efforts. He knew even before the climb the struggles we would encounter and made plans to prepare the way and the "feet" in advance. The journey rested in His abilities. Our willingness to yield opened doors of Heaven in each step we took. All He desired was trust. The remainder rested in Him.

As our paths in life toward Christ-likeness appear full of craggy rocks, small steps, and rugged places, we must trust Him to provide the means and the support for each step. After all, we are "His workmanship." Desiring our complete trust in Him as we journey through this foreign land, He calls to us and says, "Beloved, I am here to supply all you need to make it to the top. Everything necessary for your spiritual walk will be met in Me. But the greatest challenge still lies ahead. For now, I will send you back to the valley where, I will again supply all you need. I have already prepared your places to serve and stocked the supplies. I will give you the feet you need to do my work. Don't doubt. But believe." (Eph. 2:10)

IN THE VALLEY, I WILL REJOICE IN GOD, MY SAVIOR

The work can be tedious. Remember raising those children - it isn't always exciting and full of fun activities. But He called you to raise those precious vessels for Him. Keep your eyes on Him. He will lead and guide you through each challenging day as you draw them closer to Him.

What about that job and the boss or other employee you can't tolerate. Are you praying? Are you asking the Lover of your soul what YOU are to learn? What is He trying to teach YOU? When your stamina is gone and your tolerance has reached its limit, do you call on the One from whom all strength comes?

With sick parents or critically ill children - do you question His goodness and wonder how a God of love could allow it to happen? Or do you submit to His sovereign, eternal will and ask Him to help you accept the good that is to come? Are you willing to "rejoice in God, my Savior" in the heat of the struggle, or do you desire to throw in the towel. The first is of God, the second a tool of Satan. Don't let him win. "Submit yourselves, then to God. Resist the devil and he will flee from you.   Come near to God and he will come near to you." It's a promise. Claim it! (James 4:7,8a)

Life isn't easy. Jesus never promised it would be. In fact, He predicted the opposite. "I have told you these things, so that in me you may have peace. In this world you will have trouble. But take heart! I have overcome the world." (John 16:33)

He did give us a Haven of safety, a Light to brighten our path, and a solid Rock to stand on - Himself. Supporting us with constant care and shielding us in His everlasting arms, He carries us upward and onward with strong, mighty wings - the wings of an eagle.

Jesus loves you. You are His bride and a salt to others. Each day you awake, no matter your current condition, praise Him for being your Sovereign Lord. Focusing on the cross, He takes you on the heights. As His mighty streams of living waters flow through you, allow Him to touch the lives of others for Him. Then they too will experience the miracles of Heaven for they will see Christ in you.

"This is love: not that we loved God, but that he loved us and sent his Son as an atoning sacrifice for our sins. Dear friends, since God so loved us, we also ought to love one another. No one has ever seen God; but if we love one another, God lives in us and his love is made complete in us." (1 John 4:10-12) "(Jesus said), 'I have told you this so that my joy may be in you and that your joy may be complete.'" (John 15:11)

"In this you greatly rejoice, though now for a little while you have had to suffer grief in all kinds of trials. These have come so that your faith - of greater worth than gold, which perishes even though refined by fire - may be proved genuine and may result in praise, glory and honor when Jesus Christ is revealed." (1 Peter 1:6,7)

"Let us fix our eyes on Jesus, the author and perfecter of our faith, who for the joy set before him endured the cross, scorning its shame, and sat down at the right hand of the throne of God. Consider him who endured such opposition from sinful men, so that you will not grow weary and lose heart." (Heb. 12:2,3)Brunette - Heaven's Sake

DEVOTIONS FOR CHAPTERS

Chapter 1

OUR FORTRESS HAVEN OF SAFETY

"He who fears the Lord has a secure fortress, and for his children it will be refuge." (Pr. 14:26)1. Desiring to create safe environments for our children, we discover two promises in this passage. Name them. What is the one requirement on our part? What does it mean to "fear the Lord," and how can we develop that "fear". See Proverbs 2:1-8.2. How can the following verses help us in building God's fortress around our family?

2 Cor. 10:4 *The weapons of warfare are mighty through God*
Col. 3:12-17 *Loving one another doing in all in Jesus name*
Col. 4:2 *Continue in prayer & thanksgiving*
1 Peter 5:6-11 3. *Be humble, give all glory to God*

How can faith in Christ's death and resurrection build a wall of safety around our own weak and vulnerable self-esteem?

Rom. 8:1-3a *Christ has fullfilled the law for us*
Phil. 1:9-11 *Being filled with the fruits of righteousness*
Heb. 9:12-14 *The blood of Christ cleanses us for eternity*
Heb. 10:22,23 *Be faithfull without wavering*

MEDITATION: Read Psalm 46. As you do so, rest in the security found within God's fortress. Then "be still" before Him as His Spirit renews, revitalizes, and rebuilds your faith in Him through the inner man.

PRAYER: Jesus, You are my fortress and strength, an ever-present help in trouble. Help me to rest in that truth as I open my eyes to the love Christ Jesus offers today. Amen.

Chapter 2

A LIGHT TO MY PATHDIGGING INTO HIS WORD

1.   But the full light of Christ's presence will not remove the shadows until our hearts, mind and spirit open to His full radiance - the radiance of God's glory. Releasing control of our lives (surrender, humility, submission) into the loving hands of Christ remains a major obstacle for us. Why is it such a difficult step? What is God's promise to those who willingly do so?

Ps. 25:9
Ps. 149:4
Pr. 3:24
Heb. 12:9-11
James 3:17 & 4:7-8.102.

How can looking at the full light of Christ's presence and radiance remove the shadows from our lives?

John 12:46
2 Cor. 4:6
Eph. 3:16-19
1 Tim. 6:15,16
1 John 1:5-7

What do you need to remove in your life in order to fully accept that radiance?

3.   "For he has rescued us from the dominion of darkness and brought us into the kingdom of the Son he loves, in whom we have redemption, the forgiveness of sins." (Col. 1:13,14) God desires that we live in His light, walk in His light, and shed His light to others. Based on this verse, what divine blessings do we receive when dwelling daily on the kingdom of His Son, the kingdom of light? What other blessings do we receive?

2 Sam. 22:29
Ps. 27:1
Ps. 36:9
Ps. 56:13
Matt. 5:14-16
John 8:2

MEDITATION: God's light is embraced through His word. Dwell on the significance of His word in your search for the Light.
Ps. 19:8
Ps. 119:105
Pr. 6:232
Peter 1:19

PRAYER: Dearest Jesus, You truly are the Light of the world. In You and through You, my darkness will fade and the light of Your truth prevail. May Your Spirit create the desire to seek You. Provide the power to receive an enlightened spirit that I may serve You better each day. Amen.

Chapter 3

THE SALT OF THE EARTHDIGGING INTO HIS WORD

1.   I cannot help but wonder if unbelievers face many Christians today and inquire as to what spices are consumed. The grunts, the groans, the sour attitudes, the bitter spirits reflected in our faces, actions and reactions certainly indicate the flavoring that invades our hearts and minds. We need to ask if we are seasoned with hot peppers, syrupy sugar or savory salt.At times, we are all seasoned with hot peppers, syrupy sugar and savory salt. List a time below when you reflected the following attitudes.Hot peppers -Syrupy sugar - Savory salt - What was the end result of each? 2.What could you have done to change that hot pepper mentality? What steps will you take to change your reactions in the future? Compare your answer to:

Pr. 15:12
Cor. 10:5
Eph. 4:26-27.32
James 1:193.

        Pride is the center of syrupy sugar, whether in circumstances we create or in our acceptance of it from others. (See John 12:42, 43) How can focusing on Christ as the source of salt create the positive changes we need?

Ps. 16:7,8
Ps. 19:6,7
Ps. 25:15, 20-21
Rom. 5:1-2,8

Rom. 6:13
Eph. 1:13,144.

Savory salt is the desired spice of life. Compare Col. 4:6 to 1 Peter 3:15. What common thread do you observe in these two passages regarding a well-seasoned life? What is the reason for the hope that you possess? Compare your answer to Titus 2:13,14 and 1 John 3:1-3.5.Through Christ, "the everlasting covenant of salt" (Num. 18:19), we are privileged to become the salt of the earth to others. Read the following passages to discover how we can do that.

1 Cor. 2:1-52
Cor. 2:14-162
Cor. 12:8-10
Eph. 5:2
Eph. 6:18
Phil. 4:8-9

MEDITATION: In order to preserve the salt in our life, His Word must dominate our hearts and minds. Study these sections of Psalm 119 and pray that God will create the same deep, sincere love for His Word and His presence found therein.Verses 9-16Verses 33-40Verses 97-105

PRAYER: Father, as I commit my heart and soul to Your Word, use it to salt my life. Only in Your presence will I then be the effective salt that you desire. Grant me, through Your Spirit, the ability to spread the salt of Your gospel to others that You may be glorified. Amen.

Chapter 4

JESUS THE ROCK -A SOLID GROUND TO STAND ON

1.   Living in California for six years, earthquakes existed as commonplace. However the big Northridge Earthquake in 1991 shattered our casual reaction to its effects. Many homes surrounding ours encountered trashed kitchens, broken glass and cracked chimneys. Trailers slipped off jacks, fires erupted and electricity, water and gas to homes ceased for a long as six weeks.But homes on solid rock, such as ours, seemingly experienced less damage than those on fill-land. While a "whole lot of shaking" occurred, little damage inside or out could be found. The rock stood firm as did our lives and possessions that rested in His hands. A "whole lot of shaking" often occurs in our lives whether through tragedy or simply through frayed nerves and overwhelming schedules. What comfort do we have in knowing our lives rest on the Solid Rock, Jesus?

Deut. 32:4
Ps. 27:5
Ps. 62:7,8
Ps. 61:1,21
Peter 2:4,52.

What promise for resting on the rock can be found in Scripture?

Ps. 18:31,32
2 Thess. 2:16,171
Peter 5:10.113.

"You also like living stones, are being built into a spiritual house to be a holy priesthood, offering spiritual sacrifices acceptable to God through Jesus Christ." 1 Peter 2:5 You are a living stone...being built into a spiritual house. Who makes you alive according to verse 4? What do you think the words "being built" infers? Is God's work ever complete in us? As a "holy priesthood", what do we offer to the Lord? List some examples of "spiritual sacrifices."

4.   As God's living stones, perfected by Him, gradually smoothed of the rough edges, we are called to declare. What are we to declare according to 1 Peter 2:9?

MEDITATION: Read and memorize Is. 26:3,4. As you concentrate on its blessings, ask the Holy Spirit to grant the trust needed in the Rock eternal.

PRAYER: Dear Father, my Mighty Rock of Ages, send Your Holy Spirit into my heart that I may rest all my concerns on You. As I seek your face, grant me the solid ground in You that I desire. Amen.

Chapter 5

THE LIVING WATERDIGGING INTO HIS WORD

1.   If, in our lives, we seek dry river beds, such as joys of this world, eventually it will force us to erupt in hopelessness, despair and depression. The result is stagnant, unhealthy conditions that may be worse than the dry bed itself. Describe a time in your life that you experienced a dry or stagnant river bed. What was the final outcome?

2.   Our God provides an abundant supply of living water. Read the following verses and list the rewards of pursuing His water.

Ps. 36:8,9
Ps. 42:8
Is. 33:21,22

3.   Jesus described the divine blessings of His living water. Read John 7:37.38 and John 4:13.14. List those blessings. Who is the Source according to John 7:39?

4.   But as endless as the rivers, His love will pour forth. As constant and predictable as the waves, His mercies will not fail those who turn to Him in love. How do you feel knowing that His love and His mercies never fail? List ways you can respond in gratitude.

MEDITATION: What personal battles do you struggle with that often cease the flow of His ever-living stream? What can you do to restore the flow again? Compare your answer to Ps. 36:8,9.

PRAYER: Jesus, as You provide Your spring of water, welling up to eternal life, grant me the willingness to indulge in its cleansing and refreshing qualities. May Your presence quench my thirsting soul and heal my aching heart. In Your name. Amen

Chapter 6

THE APPLE OF HIS EYE-A GARDENER'S DELIGHT

1.	Being a retired teacher, the "apple of His eye" conjures up many wonderful memories. While such a simple object, it revealed a beautiful sign of affection from a child. It embraced me like a warm hug from a special agent of God. What is your definition of "the apple of His eye"? Do you perceive yourself as a beautiful sign of God's affection?

2.	We are hand picked, polished and nurtured by the Divine Gardener. Read the following verses that confirm His overseeing love for us.
Deut. 32:9.10
Is. 41:9b,10
Is. 55:12
Is. 58:14
Eph. 1:17-21
James 1:17,18

3.	We are holy and blameless, not because we did anything to deserve it, but because He passed it on to us by the cross. No one else could achieve it. Only the Resurrected Christ. Polished with His love, His cross now provides the shine, the appeal. How does He desire that we use that appeal?

2 Cor. 2:14-162
Cor. 5:18-201
John 4:71
John 5:1-54.

Eph. 1:5 reveals that, not only are we hand picked, we are adopted through "Christ Jesus in accordance with his pleasure and will." Did you realize that you are a delight to Him? What spiritual blessings can you award the One who created you for His pleasure and will? Read Eph. 1:3-8

MEDITATION: A polished apple, however beautiful, will eventually rot and decay. This, however, is not true of the "apple of His eye." As you read 1 Peter 1:3-7, write what each of the following promises mean to you.Given a new birth into a living hope -Given an inheritance that can never perish, spoil or fade - kept in Heaven for you -That through faith (you) are shielded by God's power -That your faith (is) of greater worth than gold.

PRAYER: Dear Father, thank You for the privilege of being one of Your hand picked, nourished and blessed "apples". As Your good, kind Spirit feeds me, may I respond in acts of generosity to You and to others. Amen

Chapter 7

AT HIS RIGHT HAND - ETERNAL PLEASURES

1.   Thinking we are secure in our own persons to tackle the icy roads of life, we move onward depending on our own strength. Name some times when you tried to tackle the icy roads on you own strength. What was the result? Looking back, what would you have done differently?

2.   "For I am the Lord, your God, who takes hold of your right hand and says to you, Do not fear; I will help you." (Is. 41:13) What impact does it have on you to know that the Father's hand takes hold of you to protect you? When we are timid and apprehensive, what comfort can we find in that thought?

3.   Read Exodus 15:6, 12-13. List the areas of strength discovered at God's right hand.

4.   Eternal pleasures flow from God's right hand. What are some of those pleasures?

Ps. 16:8.11
Ps. 17:7
Ps. 21:8
Ps. 63:8
Ps. 89:13-14
Ps. 98:1
Ps. 138:7

MEDITATION: Read Ps. 139:7-12. Meditate on God's abiding love as He guides you through life and upholds you with His right hand.

PRAYER: Dear Lord, in the abundance of Your goodness, You have chosen to support and uphold me with Your right hand. May I honor Your presence in a life of praise and service. Amen

Chapter 8

GOD'S EVERLASTING ARMS -REDEMPTION THROUGH SACRIFICE

1.   As the mother of four children, I remember fondly the joy and pleasure of carrying my young children. Their apparent security as well as my joy in holding them close captures my heart as one of my greatest privileges in life. Understanding that, explain God's reaction to "holding" us based on Is. 40:10-11.

2.   Jesus outstretched arms on the cross procured salvation for all. Yet not all willingly surrender to those arms, which could bear us up. What do you perceive as the greatest deterrent for acceptance? What can we personally do to encourage others to yield to His everlasting arms?

3.   Jesus is our Good Shepherd. His greatest joy and privilege is to find and restore His precious sheep. Carrying them gently in His arms, He places them in the fold of His Father. What supreme sacrifice did He make for His sheep according to John 19:14-15? What special promise is given to His true sheep in John 10:27-29?4.In gratitude for His protecting, undergirding arms, God desires that we

______________________________.

(See. Ps. 98:1) God's greatest revelation through the use of His outstretched, mighty arm is ________________. (See Ps. 77:15)

MEDITATION: Consider the power of redemption, salvation, and the abundant life offered in His loving arms. Use the following verse as you wallow in that power through wisdom.

John 3:36
John 5:24
John 6:40
John 17:3
Eph. 3:20-21

PRAYER: Dearest Jesus, the Source of all redemption, carry me in Your loving arms as I consider all that You have done for me. As You carry me through my sorrows, grief and troubles, grant me your strength and joy as I endure all for You. Amen

Chapter 9

THE SHADOW OF YOUR WINGS - SOARING TO THE HEIGHTS

1.   "I said, 'Oh, that I had the wings of a dove! I would fly away and be at rest.'" Ps. 55:6 God desires that we rest our weary souls upon Him. As you refer to the following verses for confirmation, take comfort in His protecting wings.

Ex. 33:14
Ps. 33:22
Ps. 62:5
Ps. 63:6-7
Ps. 91:1,4

2.   Read Matthew 23:37. Jesus verbally expressed His desire to gather His children together, "as a hen gathers her chicks under her wings." What prevented it? Jesus desires our closeness, our intimacy from snuggling under His wing. If you understood His intimacy as a protecting factor in your relationship, what would you do to develop more quality time in His presence?

3.   "Where do I go now, Lord? I need a resting place. I need a place to feel warm and cozy and to be refreshed. Show me that place."When was the last time you encountered that need for a hiding place? Where did you finally encounter "rest" and what was its end result? What comfort can you discover by hiding under God's wings? Refer to Ps. 61:1-4.

MEDITATION: Read Is. 40:28-31. List all the blessings that abound by finding rest in Him. List all those things you would do while soaring on eagle's wings. Then pray that you accept His strength in doing so.

PRAYER: Dear Father, help me to soar above my worries and concerns by first finding security under the shadow of Your wings. When the daily routines or harried schedules overwhelm, send Your Spirit to calm my fears and remind me of the strength in You that is there for the asking. In Jesus' name. Amen

Chapter 10

HIS BRIDE -HOLY AND BLAMELESS IN HIS SIGHT

1.   In this world of abuse, misguided thinking and inappropriate behaviors in relationships, viewing Christ as our loving Bridegroom can restore our erred thinking. His presence in our painful circumstances opens doors of growth. Inner peace results.In reading Hosea 2:19-20, what spiritual blessings do we receive in our marriage relationship to Christ?

2.   First covering of love - (Jesus) has an "Open heart-Open home" philosophy...Giving of Himself in spiritual torment and anguish on the Calvary cross, His heart cried out to us to accept the full forgiveness and new life offered between the two thieves.How does this picture of Christ effect your willingness to accept His forgiveness and new life? Read Hebrews 9:14-15 to reaffirm the ultimate sacrifice paid to redeem you.

3.   Second covering of love - Read Titus 3:4-7. Take note of the following words and describe your personal definition of each.
rebirth____
renewal____

poured out ____
generously ____
justified____
heirs____

4.   Third covering of love - "Those who look to him are radiant; their faces are never covered with shame." Ps. 34:4-5. Being reassured of His cleansing in your life, know that you are free from stain, wrinkle or blemish and are radiant in His love. Refer to the following verses for confirmation.

Ps. 25:3a
Rom. 8:1
Eph. 1:4
Phil. 2:14-16
Col. 1:22-23
1 Thess. 5:23,24

5.   Fourth covering of love - Our Bridegroom awaits our call. He yearns to provide for, to care for and to supply all our needs. He simply asks is that we trust Him and that we seek His face. List below those things that hinder your trust and prevent you from seeking His face. What steps can you take to change it?

MEDITATION: Read Psalm 45. Understanding this Psalm to be a wedding song, accept David as a "type" of Christ. It reflects His love toward us and our relationship to Him. When reading verses 1-8, visualize Christ, the Bridegroom. Then accept verses 9-17 as our relationship to Him.

PRAYER: Dear Jesus, my precious Bridegroom, I praise You for Your faithful love and commitment to me, Your bride.

Open my eyes to Your coverings of love as I seek Your presence daily. Amen

Chapter 11

FEET OF A DEER -CLIMB THE MOUNTAINS TO SERVE IN THE VALLEYS

1.   Read Habakkuk 3:17-18. List the events in your life that cause you to relate to verse 17. What has been your reaction to these events?
_____anger_____depression_____regret_____joy_____
fear_____peace_____loneliness_____comfort_____
despair_____other
How can declaring verse 18 in your life revitalize your energy in Christ?

2.   "The Sovereign Lord is my strength; he makes my feet like the feet of a deer, he enables me to go on the heights." Hab. 3:19 The climb toward God's throne remains treacherous, risky (in the worldly sense) and painful. Yet His promise for the means and support for each step prevails. Write an example of a time God prepared the way in your spiritual climb - for example, a verse, a person, a conference, a retreat. Compare that to God's promises in:

Josh. 1:9
Ps. 42:8
Ps. 43:3-4
Heb. 13:20-21
Col. 3:16-17

3.   Upon reaching the heights, He then points us toward the valley. In the valley we are to serve others with renewed

strength in Him. Find comfort in these verses as you fulfill His ministry, prepared and planned for you.

2 Cor. 5:18-20
2 Cor. 9:8-15
Eph. 2:10
Eph. 3:20-21
Heb. 13:20-21

MEDITATION: Remembering that it is God who enables us to go on the heights, no matter our circumstances, we rejoice in His love and His strength. As you read Psalm 18:32-36, 46-49, reestablish your confidence in His power to lift you to the heights again.

PRAYER: Jesus, forever grateful for Your divine Presence in my life, I now rest at the foot of Your cross. Acknowledging Your intense love for me, I rejoice in You as my strength. Praise You, precious Jesus, for allowing me to reach the heights. Now may I never fail in my desire to serve others for You. Amen